COOPERS ROCK
BOULDERING GUIDE

Dan Brayack and Tim Keenan

FALCON GUIDES ®

GUILFORD, CONNECTICUT
HELENA, MONTANA
AN IMPRINT OF THE GLOBE PEQUOT PRESS

FALCONGUIDES®

Photos by Dan Brayack unless otherwise indicated
Maps and topo illustrations by Dan Brayack

Library of Congress Cataloging-in-Publication Data is available.
ISBN 978-0-7627-4281-3

Manufactured in the United States of America
First Edition/First Printing

WARNING:

Climbing is a sport where you may be seriously injured or die. Read this before you use this book.

This guidebook is a compilation of unverified information gathered from many different climbers. The authors cannot assure the accuracy of any of the information in this book, including the topos and route descriptions, the difficulty ratings, and the protection ratings. These may be incorrect or misleading, as ratings of climbing difficulty and danger are always subjective and depend on the physical characteristics (for example, height), experience, technical ability, confidence, and physical fitness of the climber who supplied the rating. Additionally, climbers who achieve first ascents sometimes underrate the difficulty or danger of the climbing route. Therefore, be warned that you must exercise your own judgment on where a climbing route goes, its difficulty, and your ability to safely protect yourself from the risks of rock climbing. Examples of some of these risks are: falling due to technical difficulty or due to natural hazards such as holds breaking, falling rock, climbing equipment dropped by other climbers, hazards of weather and lightning, your own equipment failure, and failure or absence of fixed protection.

You should not depend on any information gleaned from this book for your personal safety; your safety depends on your own good judgment, based on experience and a realistic assessment of your climbing ability. If you have any doubt as to your ability to safely climb a route described in this book, do not attempt it.

The following are some ways to make your use of this book safer:

1. Consultation: You should consult with other climbers about the difficulty and danger of a particular climb prior to attempting it. Most local climbers are glad to give advice on routes in their area; we suggest that you contact locals to confirm ratings and safety of particular routes and to obtain firsthand information about a route chosen from this book.

2. Instruction: Most climbing areas have local climbing instructors and guides available. We recommend that you engage an instructor or guide to learn safety techniques and to become familiar with the routes and hazards of the areas described in this book. Even after you are proficient in climbing safely, occasional use of a guide is a safe way to raise your climbing standard and learn advanced techniques.

3. Fixed Protection: Some of the routes in this book may use bolts and pitons that are permanently placed in the rock. Because of variances in the manner of placement, weathering, metal fatigue, the quality of the metal used, and many other factors, these fixed protection pieces should always be considered suspect and should always be backed up by equipment that you place yourself. Never depend on a single piece of fixed protection for your safety, because you never can tell whether it will hold weight.

In some cases, fixed protection may have been removed or is now missing. However, climbers should not always add new pieces of protection unless existing protection is faulty. Existing protection can be tested by an experienced climber and its strength determined. Climbers are strongly encouraged not to add bolts and drilled pitons to a route. They need to climb the route in the style of the first ascent party (or better) or choose a route within their ability—a route to which they do not have to add additional fixed anchors.

Be aware of the following specific potential hazards that could arise in using this book:

1. Incorrect Descriptions of Routes: If you climb a route and you have a doubt as to where it goes, you should not continue unless you are sure that you can go that way safely. Route descriptions and topos in this book could be inaccurate or misleading.

2. Incorrect Difficulty Rating: A route might be more difficult than the rating indicates. Do not be lulled into a false sense of security by the difficulty rating.

3. Incorrect Protection Rating: If you climb a route and you are unable to arrange adequate protection from the risk of falling through the use of fixed pitons or bolts and by placing your own protection devices, do not assume that there is adequate protection available higher just because the route protection rating indicates the route does not have an X or an R rating. Every route is potentially an X (a fall may be deadly) due to the inherent hazards of climbing—including, for example, failure or absence of fixed protection, your own equipment's failure, or improper use of climbing equipment.

There are no warranties, whether expressed or implied, that this guidebook is accurate or that the information contained in it is reliable. There are no warranties of fitness for a particular purpose or that this guide is merchantable. Your use of this book indicates your assumption of the risk that it may contain errors and is an acknowledgment of your own sole responsibility for your climbing safety.

CONTENTS

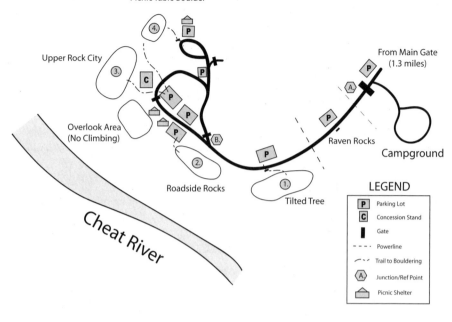

Picnic Table Boulder

Upper Rock City

From Main Gate
(1.3 miles)

Overlook Area
(No Climbing)

Raven Rocks

Campground

Roadside Rocks

Tilted Tree

Cheat River

LEGEND

P	Parking Lot
C	Concession Stand
▮	Gate
- - - -	Powerline
⌒⌄	Trail to Bouldering
Ⓐ	Junction/Ref Point
⌂	Picnic Shelter

PREFACE

The first time I came to Coopers Rock, I got hopelessly lost. I wondered around aimlessly, trying to find some rock to climb. Where I found myself (Street Fighter) turned out to be a piddly choss pile. However, with this first experience a seed was planted that, six years later, has blossomed into this book before you.

When I came to Morgantown as a freshman, I began to draw and write descriptions for problems in the Roadside Area. My first online guide was uploaded to my Yahoo! GeoCities Web site (still available in fact). With this online guide and the several that followed, I found myself faced with much cohesion and negative attitudes from the local climbing community. However, as I grew in both age and wisdom, I learned to disregard the threats and otherwise negative opinions of others.

The purpose of this guide is to expose the climbing community to a small selection of the vast bouldering at Coopers Rock State Forest.

Do not forget to enjoy yourself. Bottom line. There is no other reason to boulder or climb or run or bike or kayak or whatever. If you aren't having fun, you should find something else that makes you happy!

Be sure to be responsible and be a good steward of the land. Coopers Rock is a beautiful forest. Keep it that way. If you see trash, pick it up. If you see someone who is out of line, do not be afraid to say something.

I have to admit, the bouldering grades at Coopers Rock can be stiff. In fact, we locals get a warm feeling every time someone complains about our grades. But just have fun! Leave egos and expectations at the door; find some nice rock and just flow.

—Dan

There are too many boulder problems. I can't remember them all. I've been to countless boulder fields all over the country and even on foreign soil. But I will never forget the first boulder problem I did at Coopers Rock. It's called Golf Course. Sure, it is nothing more than a warm-up, and an easy one at that. But nevertheless, it was utterly life changing. The second I topped out that boulder problem, the rest became history. Days upon days were spent scouring the hillsides scoping out lines. Countless hours were spent trying the same moves over and over again. The first project I ever had was at Coopers Rock. The most memorable ascents have been at Coopers Rock. The best days of my life were spent bouldering at Coopers Rock.

And now the time has come to share that with others. After I started frequenting the forest, I began giving tours. People would ask me if there's a guide for this place and the response was always "You're looking at him." You could easily lose yourself in the vast complexity of the boulder fields. Hitching up with a local was always the surest way to see the best lines or the latest classic. But with the passing of time, it became more obvious that a complete, comprehensive guide was needed. A guide that would allow anyone to tour the forest at their own pace and to see for themselves how much potential it contained. But what you hold in your hands is not just a guide. It is a record of history. It is a record of time and memories, pain and sacrifice, falls, and ascents. It's a record of the amazing bouldering at Coopers Rock State Forest. While for most this will be a source of information, for a few it's a collection of the best times we've ever had.

I hope that everyone who comes to the forest will take the time to climb Golf Course. It may only take you thirty seconds out of your way. It may be at the start of your day or at the end of a long session of cranking hard. But it is a testament to the bouldering at Coopers Rock State Forest. That boulder problem changed my life. And I hope everyone can find a problem at Coopers that will do the same for them.

—Tim

Every effort has been made by the authors and editors to make this guide as accurate and useful as possible. However, many things can change after a guide is published—phone numbers and fees can change, routes can close, regulations change, facilities come under new management, and so forth.

We would love to hear from you concerning your experiences with this guide and how you feel it could be improved and kept up to date. While we may not be able to respond to all comments and suggestions, we'll take them to heart and we'll also make certain to share them with the authors. Please send your comments and suggestions to the following address:

The Globe Pequot Press
Reader Response/Editorial Department
P.O. Box 480
Guilford, CT 06437

Or you may e-mail us at:

editorial@globepequot.com

ACKNOWLEDGMENTS

When embarking on a project such as this guide, the job becomes more of an editor than an author. Guidebooks are not made by one or two people, but rather a whole community. Individuals from this community help by shaping the convoluted and often twisted thoughts of authors into a precise and respectable guidebook. Special thanks go out to this (partial) list of individuals who have turned this guide from a pipe dream into reality.

First, I will mention my climbing mentor, Bob Value, who, when I was eighteen, took me under his wing. He transformed me from a punk kid who couldn't climb 5.10 into a somewhat classy, technical, and footwork-intensive climber. He taught me to appreciate quality in not only climbing but also food, beer, guns, and women. Along with Bob, several other Pittsburgh climbers have helped turn me into a respectable member of the climbing community. Carl Samples, Mark Van Cura, and "Sponge" Bob Rentka have all contributed to my climbing, this guide, and my personality in an amazing way. Without these individuals, I would certainly be less of a person. Also, exceptional thanks to Carl for the beautifully written history and brilliant photography, as well as the wonderful days of bouldering this season; nothing's better than trying to beat a friend to an FA! (Dang Carl, you always get them first! Yum monkey-buttercups.) Without the hard-core support of my family, especially my dad, my grandpa, and my grandma (who is, in fact, a registered belayer at the Pittsburgh Climbing Wall), I would likely be stuck "diggin' holes" or something. Also, my scholastic advisor, Dr. Julio Davalos, who has helped me realize my six- (possibly seven-) year college plan. Also, if it were not for my high school conservation club sponsor, William (BRRR) Smith, I never would have found my life's passion.

Special thanks to Tim for coauthoring this guidebook with me—I couldn't have done it without you. Tim and I, up until this guide, had less-than-pleasant opinions of each other. Most of these irrational feelings were rooted, at least from my end, in jealousy of ability and fashion sense. However, this book has brought us together as friends, and as Tim spends his time in New York, I offer him best wishes and hopes that he lands his dream job with Prana someday.

The following individuals played a significant role in creating this guide: Bob Arthur, Vicky Arthur, and crew; Ryan Stocking; Young Kim; Brian Janaszek; Mike Kelly; Adam Wisthoff; Thomas McConnell; Tom Blackford; Scotty Dahl; Craig Copelin; Kurt Byrnes; Jan Kiger; and countless others.
—Dan

I would like to thank everyone who encouraged me to be the climber that I am today, first and foremost my parents, who bought me my first pair of shoes. I'd like to thank my sister for her steady encouragement. I'd also like to thank my Morgantown crew, who supported me and this project from the beginning. I'd like to thank Adventure's Edge for equipping me for my adventures. And finally I'd like to thank the Powers That Be that created all the amazing boulders we take for granted.
—Tim

City	Driving Distance to Coopers Rock (mi)	Time (hr:min)
Morgantown, W.Va.	12	0:24
Pittsburgh, Pa.	89	1:42
Fayetteville, N.C.	158	2:50
Charleston, S.C.	166	2:46
State College, Pa.	177	3:08
Washington, D.C.	200	3:21
Baltimore, Md.	208	3:23
Cleveland, Ohio	214	3:38
Columbus, Ohio	217	3:39
Lexington, Ky.	333	5:30
New York, N.Y.	375	6:14
New Paltz, N.Y.	432	7:00
El Paso, Texas	1,860	29:30
Mexico City, Mexico	2,351	39:30

INTRODUCTION

COOPERS ROCK STATE FOREST

Nestled above the Cheat River in north-central West Virginia is this little-known bouldering destination. The forest and its surrounding area is littered with "gritstone" boulders with an average height of 15 to 30 feet.

Coopers Rock has traditionally been a climbing destination. However, with the new wave of crash-pad-packing, rock-hungry boulderers, the forest has surged in popularity. Though the quality of climbing in the forest is moderate to good, bouldering is truly the best asset offered.

With its proximity to West Virginia University (Morgantown), Coopers Rock sees a diverse set of user groups, including hunters, hikers, mountain bikers, and tourists. There are many high-quality hiking and biking trails, as well as beautiful scenery and fall colors. Also, camping, picnic, and shelter-oriented facilities are provided, making the forest a popular weekend destination for tourists.

This guide only covers a small snapshot of the bouldering available in the forest. The areas listed here are generally the most developed and most convenient areas in the forest. There are, however, countless bouldering areas comparable to Tilted Tree and Roadside throughout the vast forest and surrounding areas. The areas listed in this guide are, by no means, complete representations of every possible problem or variation. The general consensus of the locals and the authors of this guidebook is: "If it's not a perfect line, then who cares!" Don't be surprised to walk through the areas and find boulders without a single established problem.

Because of the many waves of development, diversity of groups, and lack of published information, actual first-ascent and problem-name information is simply not available for many problems. Searches for information in regard to bouldering at Coopers Rock will yield little information. Until the release of this guide, there has been no formal bouldering guide to the area.

This is a challenge for a guidebook author because the information cannot be verified through recorded references. The general thought about a perceived "first ascent" is, "Someone probably has already done this problem." Hence, it is impossible to have accurate names and, even more so, to even consider first-ascent information.

A guidebook full of "unnamed" problems would be quite vague and confusing. Therefore, in this guide a query of local climbers was conducted to find a consensus of names. Some problems have three or more names. In order to be fair to each group, yet to establish a standard set of names for problems, many "aka's" ("also known as") are used throughout this guide.

Having a particular name for a problem is important for reference purposes. There are just too many (V3) arêtes out there! For example, what is *Woody's Arête* to Pittsburgh climbers is Bastard's Edge to Morgantown locals. Which of these names was assigned by a first ascentionist, if either, will likely never be answered. For the purpose of reference and in order to avoid trampling anyone's ego or ideas of the forest, problems will be

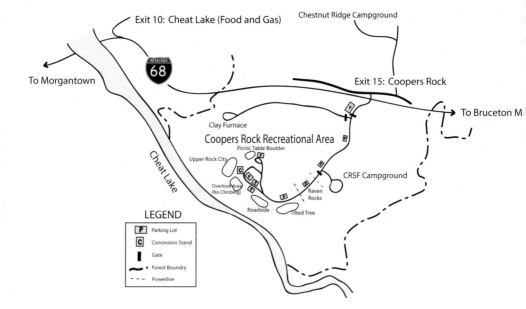

Exit 10: Cheat Lake (Food and Gas)

Chestnut Ridge Campground

INTERSTATE 68

To Morgantown

Exit 15: Coopers Rock

To Bruceton M

Clay Furnace

Coopers Rock Recreational Area

Picnic Table Boulder

Upper Rock City

Cheat Lake

Overlook Area
(No Climbing)

Raven
Rocks

CRSF Campground

Roadside

Tilted Tree

LEGEND

P	Parking Lot
C	Concession Stand
▌	Gate
∿	Forest Boundry
- - -	Powerline

assigned names that are reasonably accurate, and in multitude if necessary. For example, *Woody's Arête* (aka *Bastard's Edge*), or the *Razor Arête* (aka the *Butterfly Arête*).

ACCESS

Finding the actual forest of Coopers Rock is quite easy. The forest is located on Interstate 68 in north-central West Virginia. The nearest town is Morgantown. The best north–south access road for this area is Interstate 79, which joins I-68 in Morgantown (about 15 miles from the forest). For driving directions, view the Morgantown map at MapQuest.com, supplemented with the map provided here.

Coopers Rock is off exit 15 on I-68. Coming from Morgantown (traveling east), turn right off the exit ramp to enter the forest; traveling west (from Maryland), make a left off the exit ramp. About a quarter mile from the exit, there is a large parking lot on the right. This parking lot is used to access a good bit of the hiking and mountain-biking trails in the forest. If you continue on the road, you will pass the main gate, which will be used as a reference point for directions.

Restroom facilities are provided near the Overlook parking lot. If you choose to bring your own TP, be sure to pack it out!

The concession stand offers hot-dog-type food as well as soft drinks. For water and packaged foods, there's a well-stocked gas station at exit 10 (Cheat Lake).

ETIQUETTE

Prior to the recent influx of boulderers from the local university, Coopers Rock State Forest had been reserved as a "locals only" bouldering area. Due to the impact on and past closures of the forest, local mentality has been quite adamant and vicious in regard to guidebooks and nonlocal climbers.

With the construction of the WVU Recreational Center Climbing Wall and the recent surge in bouldering, the "local" groups at Coopers Rock have evolved from local elitists to generally friendly and social students. With this new group of climbers came much development, or at least perceived development.

Development generally is frowned upon in the forest. Since Coopers Rock is an environmentally sensitive area, please refrain from excess brushing. Absolutely do not remove trees or dig to add to a problem. There are so many good problems in the forest, it's not worth ruining the ecosystem to achieve your latest V6 POS.

Some other general tendencies to avoid are: yelling excessively loud (trust me fellows, ladies don't dig this; however, ladies, we guys love it!), chalk bag massacres, and annoying dogs. Also, music is just plain bad. *Bad bad bad!*

As far as chipping and modification of problems is concerned: Don't! Do not bring a particular problem down to your level. Instead, try to get stronger!

One important thing to consider is PR (public relations). Keep in mind that the world does not revolve around you or the bouldering community at Coopers Rock. Climbing has been closed in the forest in the past, so treat your bouldering experience as a privilege! Be polite to tourists, even if they ask you stupid questions. Let them take pictures of you, etc. Do not climb in "out of bounds" zones (The Overlook); do not disturb hunters, cyclists, or park officials; and be sure to pick up trash. Do not desecrate precious habitats to establish "Slossy Chossy" (V3), etc.

Absolutely, under no circumstances climb at The Overlook!

Try to stay on already constructed and maintained trails. At press time, adequate trails have not been established between each boulder. Make an effort to stay on trails to help reduce impact and erosion. The Coopers Rock Regional Climbers' Coalition (CRRCC) is involved in a continual process of improving trail conditions. Information about them can be found at http://coopersrockclimbers.org. If you would like to help maintain access, please contribute to the CRRCC either financially or through volunteer service.

Since 1990 the Access Fund has been the *only* national advocacy organization that keeps climbing areas open and conserves the climbing environment. The Access Fund supports and represents over 1.6 million climbers nationwide in *all* forms of climbing: rock climbing, ice climbing, mountaineering, and bouldering. More information can be found at www.accessfund.org.

HOW TO USE THIS GUIDE

This guidebook has been constructed to be as user-friendly, concise, and efficient as possible. There are several tiers of information, organized first in a broad sense and then refined.

- The forest overview map helps find specific areas.
- The general overview map helps locate the area from the parking lot(s). This includes trails, parking, and the approach.
- The bouldering-area map shows the boulder field and the grouping of specific boulders in various subareas.
- Each subarea contains a detailed map, which is explained in the accompanying text.

SYMBOLS AND ABBREVIATIONS

Maps

The maps show the problem names and grades. General "path" arrows denote approximate locations of trails.

    An arrow and number on the maps indicate the approximate start of a problem. An arrow pointing left (<) or right (>) next to the problem's name and grade indicates the direction in which the problem traverses. (For example, if you are looking

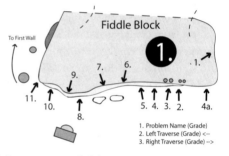

at the problem and the arrow points to the left, you traverse left.)

    Variations and problem details are not provided on most maps; problem details, including problem variations and "rules," are provided in the detailed descriptions that accompany the subarea maps. In the detailed descriptions, variations to problems are denoted with letters. Variations are only shown on the maps when they start in different locations than the original problems. An arrow indicates the start of the variation.

    Trees are denoted as circles while climbable boulders, significant roofs, and slabs are distinguished by a light-gray color. Various unclimbable reference boulders are presented in white. Generally, each significant boulder receives an "Area Boulder Number." This number is used to refer to the boulder in the detailed descriptions.

    Curved-dashed lines are used to denote the most reasonable retreat from the top of the boulders. *Note:* For all maps except the Picnic Table Boulder, the lower edges of the maps are oriented toward the river.

Topos

Photo overlays (topos) supplement area maps and problem descriptions. These overlays show the *general* path of problems and variations. Unless noted, do not follow these paths rigorously; if it makes sense to move several feet left, then move several feet left.

Text

In order to be more compact and user friendly, a set of abbreviations has been applied to the problems. These abbreviations are as follows:

- **SS = Sit-Start:** These problems begin with sit-starts or in some cases "low starts." For the most part, your rear end or back should begin on the pad(s) or ground. As long as you start on the prescribed holds, you're okay.

- **TO = Topout:** These problems finish with a topout. Most problems in the forest top out.

- **BL = Bad Landing:** Problems distinguished as those having a "bad landing" are problems that may require several spotters and/or several crash pads to adequately protect a fall. A fall from these problems could result in minor to moderate injuries. Falling would not be the end of the world, assuming you have some paddage, naddage, and spotters.

- **RBL = Really Bad Landing:** Problems distinguished as those having a "really bad landing" are problems in which a fall at the wrong place would likely result in a carry-out. A good rule for these problems is to just not fall! "RBL" has been generously assigned, so do not count a problem out until you scope the landings.

- **HB = Highball:** Highballs are problems that are generally taller than an average boulderer would be willing to "jump" or fall. However, assignment of an acceptable height is subjective. Falling off the top of a problem assigned "HB" would likely be safe with several well-placed crash pads and a spotter.

- **SHB = Super Highball:** Problems that have been assigned "SHB" are problems that are very tall. Falling off the top of these problems is generally not a good idea; a fall from one of these problems, onto one or multiple crash pads, could result in ankle, back, or other injuries. Pretty much, don't blow it up high!

GRADES AND RATINGS

Due to a runoff of climbers from Seneca Rocks and McConnell's Mill, bouldering grades at Coopers Rock have traditionally been quite stiff. Some problem grades have been adjusted to better represent "consensus" grades; however, in general, grades tend to be stiff. VB–V3 tend to be "right on." There is a big pileup at V4, and then again at V5. Also, problems rated over V6, for the most part, are probably going to be quite hard compared to national averages. Projects rated V? are really hard . . . who knows?

As with any number that defines a difficulty, there are countless definitions, conversions, and scandals. The problems in this forest are generally rated conservatively. Bouldering grades have been loosely converted to that of the Yosemite Decimal (5.10) System for rock climbing. This is like comparing apples to oranges since the two sports are quite different. An approximate conversion of bouldering grades at Coopers Rock to climbing grades in the surrounding areas is shown in the chart below, as are the number of problems for each bouldering grade.

V Bouldering	Yosemite Decimal
VB	5.7 and under
V0-	5.7-5.9
V0	5.9-5.10
V0+	5.10a/b
V1	5.10c/d
V2	5.11a/b
V3	5.11c/d
V4	5.12a
V5	5.12b/c
V6	5.12d
V7	5.13a
V8	5.13b/c
V9	5.13d
V10	5.14a

Grade	Number of Problems
VB	7
V0	46
V1	37
V2	58
V3	86
V4	67
V5	64
V6	19
V7	9
V8	2
V9	4
V10	1
V?	3
Total	**403**

A four-star system has been used to separate problems into quality groups. Of course, quality of problems is often and generally more subjective than the rating scale. Star ratings were given generously compared to problem grades. In any dispute between the authors between a star rating, the higher number was chosen. The exception to this is the four-star ratings. These were scrutinously debated among the authors until an agreement was reached.

Unfortunately for the beginning boulderer, the highest concentration of quality tends to fall in the V3–V6 difficulty range. There are, however, exceptionally high-quality moderate (V0–V2) and difficult (V7+) problems in the forest; they are just less abundant.

- **No Stars:** The crap of the crap. These problems may be listed for a "warm-up" or historical purposes. Don't bother with these problems until you've scored everything else or are feeling particularly masochistic.
- **One Star (*):** An okay problem. These problems may have good moves but may be short; or these problems may be long but have less favorable movement throughout. Other characteristics such as sharp holds, choss, or external moss may detract from the quality of these problems.
- **Two Stars (**):** These problems are the average Coopers Rock problem. Decent moves and decent height. Quite good in general.
- **Three Stars (***):** Area classics, these problems are amazing! Many of these problems have fantastic moves, coupled with high-quality rock. These problems are likely as good as four-star problems but not as popular or historically significant.
- **Four Stars (****):** As good as it gets! Great moves, bullet rock, just overall stellar! Also, these problems tend to be popular and likely contain historical significance.

Note: Problems established by the authors automatically receive at least one or two extra stars.

HISTORY

by Carl Samples

The origin of bouldering at Coopers Rock State Forest is obscure and untraceable; the thread of climbing history frays as one follows it back only thirty or forty years. Perhaps native tribal youths challenged themselves against the pocketed sandstone outcrops of the Chestnut Ridge hundreds of years ago—we will probably never know. The earliest accounts of rock climbing at Coopers Rock originate in the late 1960s and 1970s, an era when the focus of the serious climber was the lead climb, wherein the climber trails the rope and places protection en route to the top. Climbers who aspired to the challenges of granite walls in Yosemite or ice-plastered faces in the Rockies sought to make the most of these short cliffs by ascending them on lead as training. What is known of the early boulderers is that the distinction between lead climbing and unroped climbing in the '60s and '70s was often blurred. The features common to Coopers Rock cliffs, such as sloping edges and pockets, frequently afford ample purchase for fingers and shoe rubber but seldom offer secure placements for lead-climbing protection. So whether one is carrying a rack of pins and a hammer as was the norm in the sixties, or nuts and hexes for clean climbing popularized in the seventies, an intended lead climb can evolve spontaneously into a very sporting adventure, if not an outright solo.

In the original guidebook to Coopers Rock titled *Gritstone Climbs,* published in 1978, author Bill Webster indicates routes that have never been led with an asterisk. Out of 121 climbs he lists in the Overlook and Upper Rock City areas, only eleven carry the asterisk, and many of those that do not were surely solo efforts with protection opportunities that would effectively designate a rope as dead weight. The pioneering climbers of those early days at Coopers Rock almost certainly honed their mental skills as well as built a repertoire of moves on smaller boulders as they prepared for the absolute focus such serious lead climbing demanded. Records of these bouldering ascents do not exist, but names like Jeff Burns, Kevin O'Brien, Rich Pleiss, and Bill Webster would surely be among those responsible for introducing modern bouldering to Coopers Rock.

To enumerate landmark boulder problems in the forest and attempt to organize them chronologically would be a daunting if not impossible task. Assigning the names of first ascentionists would likely give birth to argument and controversy; misinformation and lack of communication are the hallmarks of bouldering activity at Coopers Rock. In the years before the current popularity of social or group bouldering, ropeless climbing was frequently the modus operandi of the lone climber. Many of the areas covered in this book were first explored with an eye for bouldering lines by single climbers simply wandering the hillsides, attracted by any outcropping of decent size. First ascents often occurred spontaneously—the purity of climbing solo with no restraints, rules, or expectations garners great rewards regardless of whether the top is attained or not. The lack of any central data compilation concerning bouldering ascents through the seventies and eighties will keep the true grit on many classics an unknown quantity forever.

Shortcomings of the historical record aside, there are a few boulder problems that represent milestones in the development of the area whose first ascents deserve mention.

Standards had been pushed into the solid 5.11 range by the 1980s (before the V scale existed), largely by two strong climbers from Pittsburgh, Don Wood and Cal Swoager. Wood's most notable efforts are the *Stevie Wonder Arête* (later known as *Colorful Corner* and now given V4) at Rock City and *Woody's Arête* (V3) at Roadside, while Swoager is best known for his first ascent of *Electric Avenue* (V4) near the Tilted Tree corridor. These two climbers are among the first who began to explore beyond the Overlook/Rock City area in search of specifically boulderable problems. Roadside provided them with the perfect venue, convenient and diverse, its potential stretching for nearly a mile, all within a few hundred yards of paved road.

The golden age of Coopers Rock bouldering could be said to have been born with the bouldering pad, as many highball test pieces were sent in the second half of the 1990s. Standards have risen steadily into the twenty-first century as climbers like Joel Brady and Brian Janaszek have done problems in the V8–V9 difficulty range, and visits by well-traveled boulderers such as John Sherman have helped Coopers Rock achieve notoriety as a world-class bouldering locale. Today, as one moves from rock to rock dropping a foam pad and pulling the shoe Velcro tight, consider that someone may have laced up and finessed that line many years ago, then silently moved on to the next challenge hidden in the forest.

TRIP PLANNING

CLIMATE AND SEASONS

Coopers Rock State Forest is closed to vehicular traffic from mid-December (after deer season) thru April 1. Hiking into the problems during this time is not suggested, although there are those who do it anyway. The forest closes every night at dark and reopens at 8 a.m.

Climate

Coopers Rock State Forest is located at a significantly higher elevation than Morgantown. This altitude, coupled with the canopy tree cover, causes the forest to be quite cool compared to Morgantown. Keep this in mind if you are checking temperatures.

Due to its proximity and generally south-facing orientation, Coopers Rock State Forest tends to dry fast. However, humidity and temperature often play significant roles in the conditions. Often, the rocks are perfectly dry the day after a heavy rain. Other times, the rocks will be soaked, even though it has not rained for weeks!

Since most of the problems in the forest are slab/face, rain-day options are limited. There are a few problems, such as the Cave Problem, that never see precipitation. Also, the Picnic Table Boulder tends to initially stay dry during a storm. However, this boulder is one of the last in the forest to dry.

Best Time to Visit

Autumn by far is the best season for bouldering. The weather is cool, the leaves are changing, bugs are nonexistent, and the rock is extremely sticky. Though the forest is often covered in a foot of snow during winter months, good friction rewards those who engage the arduous hike. Though spring is often wet, temperatures are generally manageable. Summer tends to be quite hot and humid. This weather coupled with biting insects makes summer the least favorable season for bouldering.

Plotted below are the average highs, lows, and precipitation for Bruceton Mills, West Virginia, the nearest "city" to Coopers Rock and with a similar elevation.

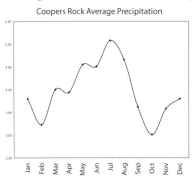

Coopers Rock Average Precipitation

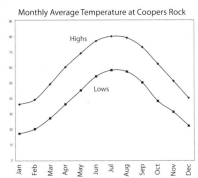

Monthly Average Temperature at Coopers Rock

SAFETY

The forest is full of dangers! Some of these dangers are, but are not limited to, rattlesnakes, copperheads, red-necks, stinging/biting insects (including deer ticks), uneven trails, loose rock, hunters, tourists, bears, rabid raccoons and bats, spiders, locals, and poisonous/hallucinogenic mushrooms (woo woo).

At all times, a boulderer must remember that he or she is not the exclusive user group of the forest. Coopers Rock State Forest is a major hunting destination, especially for deer. The number of hunters during small-game season is not excessive, however, one must be especially careful during all hunting seasons. Though Picnic Table and Upper Rock City are located in "Safety Zones," hunting is permitted in parts of Roadside and throughout Tilted Tree.

Remember, a shotgun blast to the head is fatal! First and foremost, be mindful of hunters. Be sure to make lots of "human" noises. Clipping a couple of biners or a Grigri to your crash pad or pack will alert hunters of your presence. Also, try to be considerate of hunters. In the eyes of the State, they have more of a right to be here than you.

As mentioned above, deer season brings a multitude of bloody-thirsty, high-powered-rifle-packing hunters every year. Remember, you're in West Virginia. **It is advisable to wear orange or other bright colors. Also, a dog in the woods during hunting season will likely be shot.**

The West Virginia State Hunting Seasons are as follows:

- **Small Game★:** October 8 to February 28
- **Deer (archery):** October 15 to December 31
- **Deer★ (muzzle loading):** December 12 to December 15
- **Deer (rifle)★★★:** November 21 to December 10, December 28 to December 31
- **Turkey (fall)★★★:** October 22 to November 19
- **Coyote:** No closed season

Stars indicate level of danger (with three stars being the most dangerous) to boulderers during the respective season. For a rundown on seasons, see www.wvdnr.gov/hunting/pdf/seasonsdateslimits.pdf.

EQUIPMENT

The local gear shop in Morgantown, Adventure's Edge (304-296-9007), carries a wide variety of climbing and bouldering gear, as well as a healthy stock of Prana, Patagonia, and other "New Wave" technical wear. If you need it, they probably have it.

CAMPING AND FOOD

Camping

Unless you can shack up with someone in Morgantown, your best option for camping is the Chestnut Ridge Campground (see below). The Coopers Rock State Forest campground is also available, but it's more pricy. Campground locations are found on the map on page 2.

Chestnut Ridge Park and Campground
Route 1 Box 267
Bruceton Mills, WV 26525
(304) 594-1773 or (888) 594-3111
mail@chestnutridgepark.com
www.chestnutridgepark.com

Chestnut Ridge Park and Campground is located just 10 miles east of Morgantown on Interstate 68 (exit 15/Coopers Rock). It has twenty back-in, water, and electric sites that are graveled, plus fifty wooded tent sites. Each site includes a picnic table and fire ring. RV sites are $18 per night, and tent sites are $15 per night, based on four people per site. Pets must be leashed at all times. They should not disturb other guests and must be picked up after. A refund or park credit is given for cancellations only with *written* notification, thirty days prior to the reservation date and/or if the facility is rerented.

Coopers Rock State Forest
Route 1 Box 270
Bruceton Mills, WV 26525
(304) 594-1561 or (800) CALL-WVA
coopersrock@wvdnr.gov
www.coopersrockstateforest.com

Coopers Rock State Forest has twenty-five campsites with electric hookups. Half of the sites may be reserved; the rest are rented on a first-come, first-served basis. Sites are $19 per night for four people. Hot showers are available. Pets must be leashed and cannot be left unattended. The campground is open April 1 through December 1. The camping reservation season begins the Friday before Memorial Day and ends Labor Day. If a reservation is canceled more than seven days in advance, the deposit will be refunded (except the first night's rental and a $5 handling charge).

Food

The greater Morgantown area offers a host of both high-quality and low-budget food options. The downtown Morgantown area features the most concentrated host of quality restaurants and nightlife. The easiest (but not quickest) route to Morgantown is to travel west on I-68 to exit 1. Make a left onto 119 North (Don Knotts Boulevard) and continue for about 5 miles (passing the Radisson on your left). You will find yourself entering the downtown area when the speed drops to 25 miles per hour. To avoid towing, be sure to park in pay lots or on the street.

Being a college town, there are many restaurants spread throughout the area. Each Morgantown exit contains a host of both fast-food and sit-down-style restaurants. You will certainly not go hungry in Morgantown!

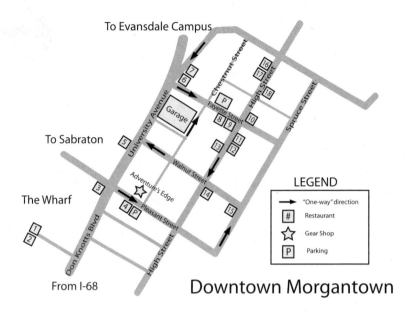

Downtown Morgantown

1. Oliverio's Ristorante: Italian, high-class.

2. La Casa: Mexican grill house, high-class.

3. Wing's Ole

4. Black Bear★: local climber/hippie hangout. Quality music, quality food, and quality beer. Wrap- and enchilada-style food with vegetarian alternatives for everything on the menu.

5. West Virginia Brew Pub: beer and drink specials seven days a week.

6. Mountain People's Kitchen: natural and organic hippie food.

7. Mountain People's Co-Op: bulk foods and other organic and natural grocery.

8. Yama★: well-priced, authentic Japanese food, mostly bowls.

9. Pita Pit

10. Subway

11. Cold Stone: high-quality ice cream.

12. Mediterranean Market: Middle Eastern groceries and deli.

13. Boston Beanery: "American" food, TVs, bar.

14. Buffalo Wild Wings: cheap wings, bar.

15. Blue Moose Café: high-quality coffee shop.

16. Casa D'Amici: decent pizza.

17. Dairy Queen

18. Quiznos: fresh subs.

(Recommended restaurants are starred.)

COOPERS ROCK

TILTED TREE

Directions: From the first gate, travel 2.1 miles to the first lot on the right after the second (and major) power line. Don't stop at the Raven Rocks parking lot; go to the unsigned parking lot beyond it. Cross the street and continue down the large, gated trail for about 150 yards. Just as the trail begins to increase grade, you will see an obvious trail on the right, which trends down and left. Follow this trail past the fallen tree to a break in the cliff line. This is the main entrance to the Tilted Tree Area.

Tilted Tree is the bread and butter of bouldering at Coopers Rock. There are scores of high-quality lines, including the super classics *Twist Dah Hick* (V5), *Moby's Dick* (V3), *Stick with It* (V5+), *Coral* (V7), the *Question Mark* (V5), plus countless others. The Tilted Tree Area has a diverse selection of problems ranging from delicate slabs to powerful roofs. For a person looking to taste Coopers Rock at its finest, look no further.

The natural clustering of the boulders in this area does not lend itself to a straightforward order of layout. The Tilted Tree Corridor is listed first because it is the most popular

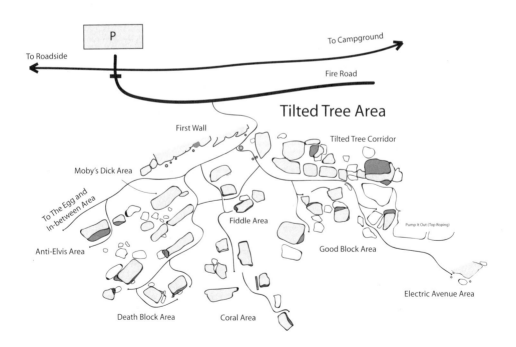

Tilted Tree Area

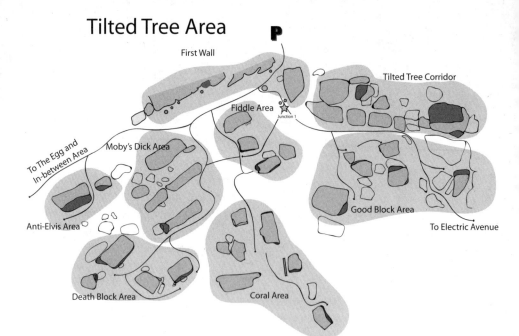

From the entrance trail, continue down past a large boulder on your left. Squeeze through two large trees, turn left at Junction 1, and continue about 30 yards until you see the three obvious boulders on your left. This is the Tilted Tree Corridor.

area. Be sure to check the overview map if you are having trouble orienting yourself. *Note:* The bouldering overview map does not include the Electric Avenue Area. This area is about 200 yards past the Good Block Area.

Heading south from the parking area, at Junction Point 1 make a left for the Tilted Tree Corridor, the Good Block Area, and Electric Avenue. These three areas are presented first. Turn right at Junction Point 1 to reach the other areas, which are presented after the Electric Avenue Area.

Tilted Tree Corridor

The Tilted Tree Corridor features a concentration of both moderate and difficult high-quality problems. *Twist Dah Hick* (V5), *Pocket Prow* (V6) and *The Bulge* (V5) are classic hard problems. Also, there are several notable moderates in this area: *The Practitioner* (V1), the *Big Pocket Problem* (V0+), the *Always Dry Roof* (V2), and *Black Scar* (V1).

Boulder 1:
Pocket Prow Boulder

1. ***Return of the Swallows: What a great problem! But don't try it unless you are solid on V1—the landing is total death! Start on a pinch and move past an edge to an incut pocket. Continue on the arête past an edge, pockets, and a pinch, finishing on the slab just right of the arête. (V1) (SS TO HB RBL)

2. *Walk-Off (aka Laid Back): Can you turn left? Start on the left arête on a right-facing jug. Follow the arête past pockets to the top. (V1) (TO)

Tilted Tree Corridor

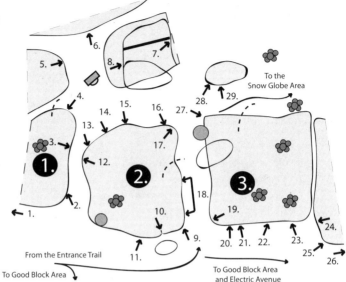

3. ****Pocket Prow: Definitely not V7 as graded in a *Rock and Ice* article! Beta varies, but establish on a low pocket and make a core-intensive move to a deep pocket. Continue with another powerful move past shallow pockets and a sloper to the top. This problem is reach dependant. (V6) (TO)

 a. ***Variation: Jump-start to the high pocket and finish as normal. (V5) (TO)

4. ***The Bulge: For such a short problem, The Bulge sure packs a punch! Start on a sloper and right-facing flake. Scum your way up the burly arête past pockets to a heart-breaker finish. (V5) (SS TO)

5. *Baby Maker: Start on two sharp pockets and move up and left to a horizontal. Finish matched on the upper lip. (V1) (SS)

6. Wet Ho's: Reported at V4 by the first ascentionist, the problem has not likely been done since. Start on pockets and make a long move past a sloper to the top. (V4) (TO)

7. ***Always Dry Roof: Step up to a jug and ascend the striking roof crack using painful yet alluring hand and foot jams. Traverse off right and downclimb. (V2)

 a. **Variation Finish: Instead of going right, make a scary, sloping lip traverse left and finish up the corner. (V4) (TO)

8. *S & M Roof: Start on two jugs on the triangular boulder. Move up past a jam in horizontal to a seam. Utilizing double heel hooks, match and hit the top. This problem is height dependant. A spotter is advised for the potential "back-flip." (V5) (TO)

Boulder 2

9. ***Black Scar: Start on a pinch and pocket just left of the arête. Continue up the left side of the arête on slopers, edges, and pockets, past a sloping layback to the top. (V1) (TO HB)

10. *Gag Reflux: Start in the middle of the block on a horn. Follow the left-facing flake and pockets to a thin move for the top. (V3) (TO HB)

11. *Rubric's Cube: Start on a large sloping jug and make a deceptively hard move to the large cannon-ball pocket. Continue past another pocket and edge to a height-dependent finish. Start-beta varies the grade. (V4/5) (TO HB)

To view the topography for problems 12 to 17, 27, and 27a, see the topo below.

12. *Two Bagger: Start on the arête and move up through sloping pockets to a thin topout. (V1) (SS TO)

13. *Prick Pocket: A "fill-in" problem that turns out to be decent. Start just left of the arête on a sharp left pocket. Move up and right to a sloping pocket on the arête. Make a long move past a shallow pocket to the top. Avoid laying back on the arête. (V4) (TO)

14. ****The Practitioner (aka The Proctologist): A super classic for the grade! Start 4 feet left of the arête on two pockets. Move up past an undercling and stick your digit as far as you dare into the pocket. Continue past another pocket, finishing right. (V1) (TO)

15. ****Big Pocket Problem (aka Belly Button): The complementary four-star moderate. Start on a pocket and pinch. Move up and left past a large pocket and through several small pockets to the top. (V0+) (TO)

16. **One Bagger: Another good "fill-in" problem. Start on a low sloper about 3 feet right of the arête. Move up and right past a pleasant pocket, a hollow edge, and another pocket to the top. (V0) (TO)

17. **Golf Course: Start on the same low sloper as the previous problem, but instead move left and follow the arête past pockets and a pinch to the top. (VB) (TO)

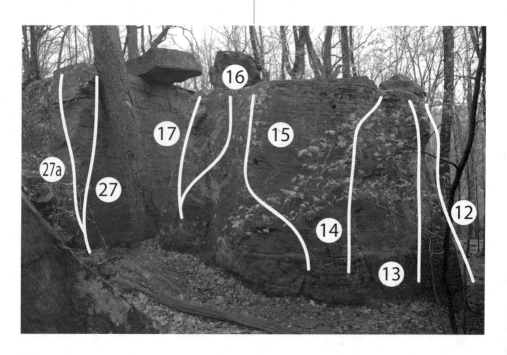

Bill Bauer coming to terms with *Big Pocket Problem.*

18. **Tilted Tree Slab: This featured slab offers many moderate and difficult eliminates. The best eliminate starts under the largest pocket on edges and avoids the large pocket as both a hand and a foot. (V0–V3) (TO)

Boulder 3

19. ****Twist Dah Hick: One of the best-looking lines in the forest, and it climbs just as well as it looks! Start on opposing sidepulls and move up to a jug. Continue out left to a pocket and ascend the clean, gently over-hanging face making several long, core-intensive moves. Though many have screamed it, this problem is definitely not height dependant. The problem was finally named by the first ascentionist after a threat of calling it the "Happy-Happy Sugar Arête." (V5) (TO HB)

20. **Visitation: A good problem, however, the hardest moves are way off the deck! Start just right of the arête on opposing sidepulls. Move through pockets and past a left-facing flake to a flat edge. Continue past a dicey sloper to the top. (V2) (HB TO)

21. ***Liquid: Start on a low incut pocket and a high shared pinch *(Visitation).* Continue past a left facing flake and sloper-edge to a horizontal. Finish right of *Visitation.* (V3) (TO)

22. **Crazy Times: Start on a pocket and bad edge. Bear down and continue through grim slab to jugs. (V7) (TO)

23. ***Sinking: Start on a mono pod and continue past a pinch pocket to a sloping horizontal. Set up with a mantel, finishing left on a jug. (V2) (TO)

24. **Occam's Razor: Try not to multiple entities unnecessarily. A perfect setup throw. Start just right of the crevice on your choice of pockets, and bomb for the top. (V5) (TO)

25. The Deer's Last Stand: This problem is not recommended in its present state, but the historical significance warrants a mention. One winter a deer fell into the crevice just left of this problem, entrapping itself. The deer froze to death, and in the spring the carcass began to decompose. The awful smell did not stop the locals from scrubbing and sending this arête (V5). The problem was named in honor of the deer.

26. **Flood: Though it doesn't look good, it climbs quite well. Start right of the tree on a high jug (jump if you must). Follow pleasant jugs up the overhanging wall. Scamper to a jug over the roof and step off left. (V2) (HB BL TO)

The next three problems are located near the large, tilted tree left of *Twist Dah Hick*.

27. **Tilted Tree Arête: Start just left of the tilted tree on two pockets. Staying on the right side of the arête, make power moves through pockets and edges to the top. (V3) (TO)

a. *Variation: Follow the left side of the arête to the top. (V1) (TO)

28. **Cooperchaun: A pun on its HP-40 twin, "Leprechaun." A great 3-foot boulder problem! Okay maybe not. Start on pockets and a heel hook "starting hold for Cletus Funk." Overcome the sloping bulge and finish with a difficult mantel. (V3+) (SS TO)

29. **Cletus Funk: How low can you go? An inquiry we made to local hardman Bob Rentka when he told us about this problem. Start on a sloper and finish with an awkward mantel. (V3) (SS TO)

Boulder 4: Snow Globe Area

To reach this set of boulders, continue up the hill past the Tilted Tree Arête. This area is distinguished by the atypical horizontal roof.

30. ***Roof Problem: The Roof has a plethora of different starts, each crescendoing

Snow Globe Area

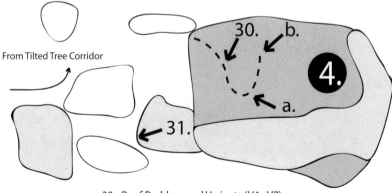

30. Roof Problem and Variants (V4 - V7)
31. Snow Globe (V8?)

in difficulty. The easiest variation is listed first: Start on a large jug on the left side of the roof and continue out through jugs and edges to the lip. Finish out the left side of the *Roof.* (V4) (TO)

a. ***Variation:** Start on an edge and heel-hook about 3 feet down and right from the normal start. Continue out through bad edges to join the normal problem. (V5) (TO BL)

b. ***Final Fantasy:** Timmy's parting contribution, and what a line! Start on a sharp incut pocket about 3 feet further back from the first variation and continue out to join it. (V7) (TO BL)

31. *Snow Globe: Rumored to be a Matt Bosley test piece. Start in the daunting hole and follow "holds" and right arête to the top. Try this one on a sunny day . . . you'll get the picture. (V8?) (SS TO RBL)

Good Block Area

The Good Block Area hosts a cluster of decent- to moderate-quality problems, as well as one of the classic hard compression problems, *Shadow Boxer* (V6).

From the entrance, continue down and left, past a large boulder on your left. Squeeze through two large trees, turn left at Junction 1, and continue about 20 yards until you see a trail on the right. This trail leads to Boulders 1 through 4. Boulder 5 can be reached by continuing on the trail past the Tilted Tree Corridor. At press time there was no set trail between Boulders 2, 3, and 4.

Boulder 1: The Good Block

The problems on the Good Block add low starts and variations to already established sport and mixed routes.

1. *Start on a rounded jug and horizontal under the left side of the roof. Move up and

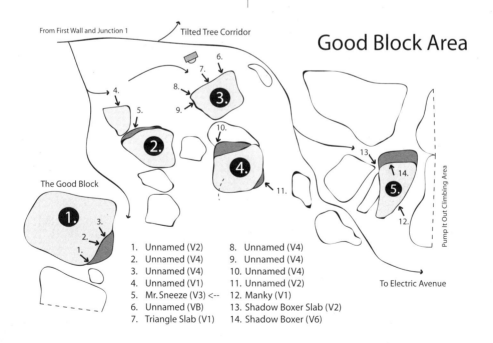

Good Block Area

1. Unnamed (V2)	8. Unnamed (V4)
2. Unnamed (V4)	9. Unnamed (V4)
3. Unnamed (V4)	10. Unnamed (V4)
4. Unnamed (V1)	11. Unnamed (V2)
5. Mr. Sneeze (V3) <--	12. Manky (V1)
6. Unnamed (VB)	13. Shadow Boxer Slab (V2)
7. Triangle Slab (V1)	14. Shadow Boxer (V6)

To Electric Avenue

right to jug on the arête. Continue past a horizontal, finishing on a slopey ledge below the triangular prow. Be sure to have a spotter, since the retreat entails downclimbing the problem and jumping. (V2) (SS BL)

    a. Variation: Start the same, but traverse low right on thin edges, joining the finish of problem 3. (V5) (SS)

2. ★★Start on edges and move out past an undercling flake to a sloper. Make a long move out left to an aloof edge and then make another long move to a horizontal to finish. (V4) (SS)

3. Start on a jug in a large pocket. Move out right on underclings and continue traversing right to a large right-facing flake. Finish on a jug horizontal about 15 feet off the deck. (V4) (SS)

Boulder 2

The start of problems 4 and 4a entail a subtle "hop" instead of a difficult establish.

4. ★Start on the fissure in the center of the face and step up and left to a jug. Finish over the top. (V1) (TO)

    a. Variation: Start the same, but step up and right to a jug. Finish over the top. (V0+) (TO)

    b. ★★**Poulder Broblem:** Start on the right side of the small face on a sloper. Continue up and left to the obvious jug from the previous variation. Heel-hooking the starting hold adds a bit of difficulty, but is aesthetic. Avoid the arête. (V2) (TO)

5. ★**Mr. Sneeze:** TK would say, "A must do at the grade!" but then it just looks like another 3-foot-high lip traverse! "It's gay" per the first ascentionist. Start hanging on the sloping lip on the right side of the boulder. Traverse

the lip left through grim conglomerate to arête and finish. (V3) (TO)

Boulder 3

To view the topography for problems 6 through 9, see the topo on p. 21.]

6. A short but good warm-up problem. Start on a large sloper and continue up and right past a right-facing sloper. Finish on the sloping arête. (VB) (SS TO)

7. ★★**Triangle Slab:** Step up on pockets and ascend the thin face, finishing over the point. (V1) (TO HB)

8. ★Start just right of the tree on a left-facing sidepull. Move up and left "avoiding the right arête" to join *Triangle Slab* near the top. (V4) (SS TO HB)

9. ★Start on the far right arête on a pinch and pocket. Scum up the left side of the arête past an edge, pockets, and a sidepull, finishing up the left side of the right arête. (V4) (SS TO HB)

Boulder 4

The best downclimb for this block is the back arête (cold shuts). Be very careful with this downclimb! You may want to consider a crash-pad-assisted "jump" from somewhere else.

10. ★★Start on a right-facing sidepull and sloper on the arête. Move up pristine right-facing flakes, finishing on the right side of the arête with a slopey topout. Blowing the topout would be fugly. (V4) (SS TO RBL)

11. ★★Start on the right side of the rising crack. Traverse left to an undercling and edge.

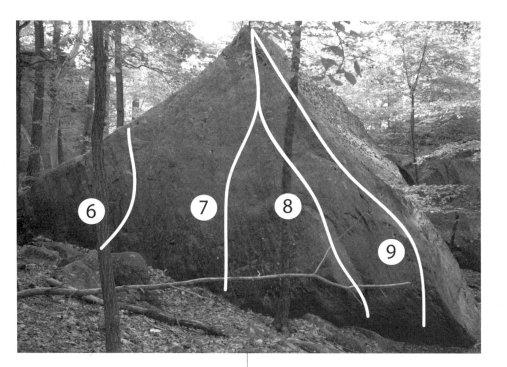

Make a long move to a "jug" and finish matched. Topping out is not advised. (V2) (SS)

Boulder 5

12. Manky: Follow the manky left-facing flake to the top. (V1) (TO)

13. *Shadow Boxer Slab: Ascend the delicate slab just right of Shadow Boxer. (V2) (TO HB)

14. ***Shadow Boxer: A perfect endeavor for the Creatine-gulping sport pilots, and definitely a bouldering-mongrel kinda problem. Two distinct sets of beta, both at the same grade. Start on the sloping arête and ascend the proud overhanging face, finishing through the benign slab. (V6) (SS TO)

Electric Avenue

The Electric Avenue Area has several high-quality established lines and potential for some very hard problems.

Continue past Shadow Boxer, passing Pump It Out (TRing area) on your left. Make a right down the hill through several boulders to a trail. Take a left on this trail and continue about 30 yards until you see a large boulder down and to the right. Follow the trail down to this boulder. This is the last boulder listed in this area to the right.

1. ***Two Minutes of Hate: It looks sharp, but its not. In fact, it's quite a good line! Start on two high incut edges and ascend the gently overhanging face past a pinch and deep edge to a textbook topout. (V3) (TO BL)

2. *Such Sunsets: A buttermilk/granite-esque, Joel Brady special. Start in front of the

Electric Avenue

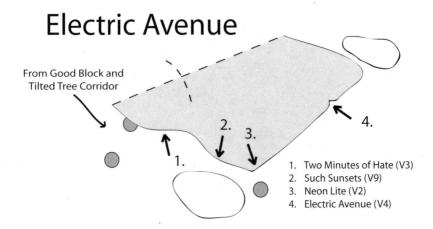

From Good Block and
Tilted Tree Corridor

2.
3.
4.
1.

1. Two Minutes of Hate (V3)
2. Such Sunsets (V9)
3. Neon Lite (V2)
4. Electric Avenue (V4)

intruding boulder on thin edges and make desperate moves past pockets, edges, and slopers to the top. (V9) (SS TO BL)

a. *Variation: Eliminates the sit-start. (V6) (TO BL)

Cal Swoager in the pre-crash-pad days on Electric Avenue. PHOTO BY CARL SAMPLES

To the right of Such Sunsets is a series of fracture flakes, which has been done but is not worth more than a mention.

3. *Neon Lite: Start on a high jug and follow the interesting features to a ledge. Continue up past a pocket to a really scary topout. (V2) (TO HB RBL)

4. ****Electric Avenue: As sweet as it gets at Coopers Rock! Ascend the striking crack to its end. Make a difficult transition out right to another crack and follow inviting finger jams to the top. This daunting line was soloed by Cal Swoager "sans crash pad" in 1984. (V4) (TO SHB)

a. ***Electric Avenue Direct: After soloing the problem, Cal Swoager walked around and promptly fired this variation. Instead of transitioning into the right crack, continue straight up. (V4) (TO SHB)

First Wall

The First Wall features a handful of low- to moderate-quality problems as well as several high-quality lines, including one of the classic problems in the forest, *The Question Mark* (V5). Christened as a gem by visiting climber John Sherman, this highball is a must-do.

As you continue down the trail from the initial entrance trail, the first line of boulders encountered is the First Wall Area. This area consists of the Squirrel Soup Boulder (Boulder 1) and the upper cliff band, which extends about 200 yards.

The First Wall has been broken into two sections: First Wall Right and First Wall Left.

Boulder 1:
Squirrel Soup Boulder

This boulder is characterized by the disproportionately tall slab. Several toprope routes have been established, including the arête Squirrel Soup (5.7).

1. *Nuts in a Branch: Start on a small pocket and power past a sloper, finishing over the top. (V2) (SS TO)

2. ***Four Ton Mantis: One of the most exciting problems in the forest. Just don't look down, or even think about blowing it! Start on the horizontal and ascend the slab through precarious pockets and smears to a frightful but straightforward move to the top. Consider rapping down and brushing for some added piece of mind. (V3) (TO SHB)

3. **Four Ton Nuts: Start on Four Ton Mantis, but follow the horizontal right to the arête. Finish by downclimbing Squirrel Soup. (V2) (HB)

4. *Kick in the Coops: It looks so harmless, but it's so hard! An old "12a" toprope route that we now just boulder to the horizontal. Start on opposing flakes and follow thin moves through the right-facing flake to the horizontal. Traverse left and downclimb the arête. (V5) (BL)

5. **Squirrel Poop: Characterized by a serious lack of feet. Start near the beginning of the slanting fissure and follow it to the Squirrel Soup Arête. Downclimb the arête. (V3) (SS HB)

6. **Flying Nut-Muncher: Super technical! Start on a sidepull and step up to pockets. Set up with a flake and engage thin moves past a mono–pinch pocket and a sloper pinch to a jug. Finish over the top. (V6) (TO HB)

Boulder 2

7. ****The Question Mark: A classic! Start on incut edges and make an enigmatic set of moves past underclings, a pocket, and an edge

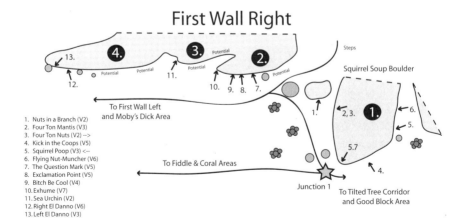

First Wall Right

13.
4.
3.   Potential
2.
Potential   Potential   Potential   Potential   Potential
12.   11.
10. 9. 8. 7.

Steps

Squirrel Soup Boulder

1. Nuts in a Branch (V2)
2. Four Ton Mantis (V3)
3. Four Ton Nuts (V2) -->
4. Kick in the Coops (V5)
5. Squirrel Poop (V3) <--
6. Flying Nut-Muncher (V6)
7. The Question Mark (V5)
8. Exclamation Point (V5)
9. Bitch Be Cool (V4)
10. Exhume (V7)
11. Sea Urchin (V2)
12. Right El Danno (V6)
13. Left El Danno (V3)

To First Wall Left
and Moby's Dick Area

To Fiddle & Coral Areas

1.
2, 3.   1.   6.
5.
5.7
4.

Junction 1

To Tilted Tree Corridor
and Good Block Area

Tim Keenan drops the toprope for *Four Ton Mantis*.

to an incut letterbox. Make scary but easy moves off the letterbox past flat edges to the top. High, but safe with a crash pad and spotter. (V5) (HB TO)

8. **Exclamation Point: A good body-tension-oriented problem. Follow layback cracks through smeary moves to a high sloper. Make a dicey move off the sloper to the top. (V5) (HB TO)

9. **Bitch Be Cool: Start on an edge (above horizontal) and make a hard move past a pocket and edge to a deep letterbox. Traverse left, making a long move to a good edge. Continue left past a pocket to a jug on the arête. Finish up the arête. (V4) (SS TO)

    a. **Variation: Eliminates the sit-start. (V3) (TO)

10. *Exhume: Start on a bad edge and pocket. Paw up and establish on a pinch and

layback. Make a long move to a jug and finish up the arête. (V7) (SS TO)

    a. **Variation: Eliminates the sit-start. Make a difficult establish and follow the arête to the top. (V3+) (TO)

Boulder 3

11. **Sea Urchin: Ascend the left-facing flake system to the top. (V2) (TO HB)

Boulder 4

12. ***Right El Danno: What a great problem! Start on opposing pockets and continue past a pocket to a sloping rail. Bomb over bulge to thin slopers and finish up the slab. (V6) (TO HB)

    a. ***Center El Danno: Start the same, but from the sloping rail, make a big move to a left-facing sidepull. Finish through slopers. (V6) (TO HB)

13. Left El Danno: Start just right of the tree on an undercling and follow the left-facing flake past sloping horizontals to the top. You may find yourself playing "twister" with the tree. (V3) (HB BL TO)

Boulder 5

To reach Boulder 5, continue down the trail for about 20 yards.

14. *Fat Girls: Start on an undercling and high pocket. Make a long move out left to a double pocket. Continue past a left-facing sidepull and horizontals to the top. (V2) (TO)

15. **Rhesus Monkey Butter Cups: You'll have to ask Carl Samples about the origin of this name! Start in a lone sinker pocket and somehow struggle past bad pockets and worse slopers to a victory bucket and easy topout. (V5) (TO)

16. *Blood Bath and Beyond: Step up to a deep two-finger pocket and continue past another pocket to a jug. Continue through jugs, stepping right to finish. The opening pockets are quite sharp. (V2) (TO)

17. *EMT on a Stick: A guy named Jeff Pesarsick established this problem while training to become an EMT. He finished this problem directly over the roof! During the time of the ascent, a daggerlike spike from the now-rotting stump was his punishment for failure. The spike is now gone, but the topout over the lip is still not recommended. Start on the right-facing flake and move up past a horizontal to a jug. Traverse left, entertaining a combat finish (scary, mossy, and loose!). (V3) (TO BL)

18. *I Dig Friction: Start just right of the arête, with a difficult establish. Ascend the slab, finishing just left of the tree. (V0) (TO)

19. **Cry Ankle: Start on a low seam just right of the chimney. Continue up, following the left side of the arête to the top. At least one ankle has been broken falling off of this one. (V3) (SS TO)

There is an easy problem that goes out the center of the roof (VB) that is not worth more than a mention.

Boulder 6

20. Stupid Crack: Ascend the short, juggy, right-facing flake to the top. This problem is also a convenient downclimb. (VB) (TO)

The standard retreat for the next problem and variants is to traverse right and downclimb Stupid Crack.

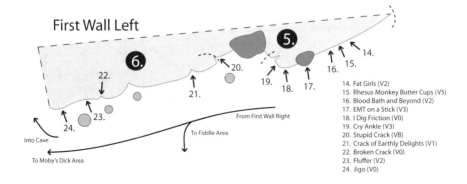

First Wall Left

14. Fat Girls (V2)
15. Rhesus Monkey Butter Cups (V5)
16. Blood Bath and Beyond (V2)
17. EMT on a Stick (V3)
18. I Dig Friction (V0)
19. Cry Ankle (V3)
20. Stupid Crack (VB)
21. Crack of Earthly Delights (V1)
22. Broken Crack (V0)
23. Fluffer (V2)
24. Jigo (V0)

Into Cave

To Moby's Dick Area

To Fiddle Area

From First Wall Right

21. **Crack of Earthly Delights: Ascend the brilliant finger crack, finishing right of the tree. (V1) (TO HB)

a. *Bosch This: Establish just right of the crack on a high, thin horizontal. Continue past a jug and thin horizontals to the top. Avoid the crack. (V3) (TO HB)

b. **Rinky Dink: Start several feet left of the crack on a left-facing flake. Move right past a sloper to a large pocket. Make hard moves through thin slopers to a horizontal, finishing just left of the crack. Avoid the crack. (V4) (TO HB)

22. *Broken Crack: Ascend the broken crack to the top. (V0) (TO HB)

23. **Fluffer: Quite a good problem. Start just right of the large tree on an edge. Make a long move to another edge and continue on horizontals to the top. Either traverse right and downclimb *Broken Crack* or top out left of the tree. (V2) (TO HB)

24. Jigo: Follow the left-facing flake system, trending left to finish on the arête. (V0) (TO HB)

Fiddle Area

The Fiddle Area hosts an overload of high-quality moderate and difficult classics. One of the gems in the forest, the Fiddle Block, has a host of high-quality slab problems for everyone. Classics on this boulder include the classic hard slab problems: *Stick with It* (V5+), the *Tombstone Arête* (V4), and the high-quality moderate *FFF* (V1). The Wave Rider Boulder (Boulder 2) features the classic must-do highballs: *Wave Rider* (V5) and *Lycrapeedium* (V4), as well as the super-classic: *Wave Crasher* (V3). The long-standing project *Love Ta Hate* (V9) was finally sent. This highball test piece will surely challenge your nerves!

From the entrance, continue down and left, past a large boulder on your left. Squeeze through two large trees, turn right at Junction 1, and continue for about 30 yards until you see a fractured, overhanging face on your right. This is the Wave Rider Boulder (Boulder 2) in the Fiddle Area.

The Fiddle Area is broken into two sub-areas: the Upper Fiddle Area (Boulders 1 and 2) and the Lower Fiddle Area (Boulder 3).

Boulder 1: Fiddle Block (aka Hall of Fame Boulder)

1. *Fiddlesticks: Just too beautiful a face to not have a problem! A little contrived, but quite subtle. Step up to a sloper and move left to a small pocket. Power off the pocket to the top, finishing left. (V3) (TO)

Dan Brayack cruxing on *Fiddlesticks*.

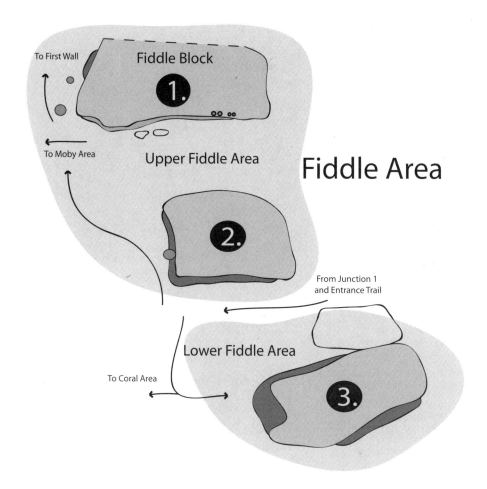

Fiddle Area

To First Wall

Fiddle Block

1.

To Moby Area

Upper Fiddle Area

2.

From Junction 1
and Entrance Trail

Lower Fiddle Area

To Coral Area

3.

2. ***FFF (Fiddle Finger of Fate): What a great moderate! Start on low jugs and step up to an undercling. Continue past edges and a technical high-step to the top. (V1) (TO)

3. *Second Fiddle: A decent moderate problem and also the most convenient down-climb. Start below the fissure and follow the plethora of edges, pockets, and jugs to the top. (VB) (TO)

4. ***The Fiddle: Easier until the "Fiddle" broke. Start just left of the previous problem on a jug foot and right-facing edge. Continue through thin holds, past the "Fiddle," to a good pocket and the top. (V3) (TO)

5. **Sloping Rail: Another creative name; the companion V3 warm-up on the Fiddle Block. Start just left of the Fiddle on a right-facing edge. Make a thin move on bad feet and follow the sloping rail up and left to the top. (V3) (TO)

To view the topography for problems 6 through 11, see the topo on p. 29.

6. ****Stick with It: The classic hard slab problem in the forest! So thin, yet so good! Locate a high pinch in front of the first protruding talus. Start beta varies, but establish on underclings, a shallow left pocket, or an

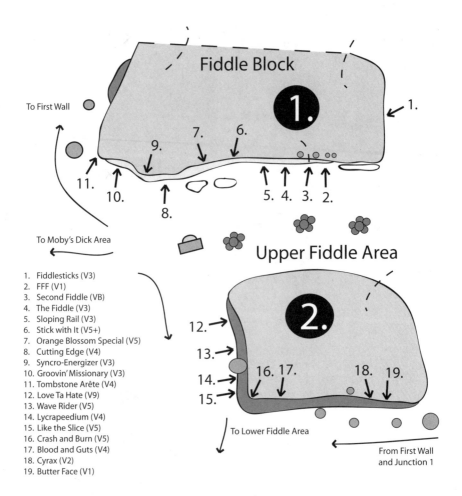

Fiddle Block

To First Wall

1.

1.

7.   6.
9.

11.
10.

5. 4. 3. 2.

8.

To Moby's Dick Area

Upper Fiddle Area

1. Fiddlesticks (V3)
2. FFF (V1)
3. Second Fiddle (VB)
4. The Fiddle (V3)
5. Sloping Rail (V3)
6. Stick with It (V5+)
7. Orange Blossom Special (V5)
8. Cutting Edge (V4)
9. Syncro-Energizer (V3)
10. Groovin' Missionary (V3)
11. Tombstone Arête (V4)
12. Love Ta Hate (V9)
13. Wave Rider (V5)
14. Lycrapeedium (V4)
15. Like the Slice (V5)
16. Crash and Burn (V5)
17. Blood and Guts (V4)
18. Cyrax (V2)
19. Butter Face (V1)

2.

12.

13.

14.   16. 17.   18. 19.

15.

To Lower Fiddle Area

From First Wall
and Junction 1

edge. Rail off "imaginary" edges to "imaginary" slopers. Balance on a sharp sidepull and make a balancey move past a good pinch, finishing with a dicey move for the top. (V5+) (TO BL)

7. *Orange Blossom Special: Start on inward-opposing sidepulls just left of *Stick with It* above the "death" talus. Make a hard first move and continue through easier moves to the top. (V5) (TO BL)

8. **Cutting Edge: Start just right of the orange streak on a sidepull. Move out right past another sidepull and make a long move

for a sharp iron edge. Follow dicey but positive edges to the top. (V4) (TO HB BL)

a. Variation: Adds the sit-start. (V4+) (SS TO BL)

9. *Syncro-Energizer: Start just left of the previous problem on a shared pinch and jug. Follow the thin, thought-provoking seam past sidepulls to a sloper. Monkey off the sloper to the top. (V3) (TO HB)

10. Groovin' Missionary: Start several feet right of the arête on a pinch and pocket. Move up and left past edges, a pocket, and a hollow undercling to the top. (V3) (TO HB)

11. ***Tombstone Arête: A great arête problem. Start on a sharp pinch and ascend the left side of the arête, moving past a pocket and pinch to the top. "Tricky" beta makes this problem manageable. Unless you're really silly, you probably won't hit the tree. (V4) (TO BL)

    a. **Variation: Adds the sit-start. (V4+) (SS TO BL)

Boulder 2:
Wave Rider Boulder

12. ***Love Ta Hate: This long-standing project was finally sent by visiting climber Ivan Green, but not before an exciting throw, miss, and fall from the top! Start on a jug and ascend the desperate face, moving past an undercling, pockets, and a sloping rail to a desperate finish. (V9) (TO SHB)

Ivan Greene on the first ascent of *Love Ta Hate*.

13. ****Wave Rider (aka Riding the Crest of the Wave): A great highball. Start on low edges and make a long move to a jug. Continue with burly moves through the railroad edge, past a pinch to a devious horizontal. Finish with a sketchy topout. Most people use casual leg-hip-tree contact for the topout. (V5) (SS HB TO)

    a. ****Variation: Eliminates the sit-start. (V4) (SS HB TO)

14. ***Lycrapeedium: Wow! It's amazing that this line remained undone for so long! Start on a low pocket in front of the tree and pimp through sharp pockets. Make a committing move out left (watch the tree) to sidepulls and continue past a sloper, pocket, and undercling to a sobering topout. Try not to pee your Lycra. (V4) (SS TO HB BL)

15. Like the Slice (aka Red Dawn): Start on a left-facing sidepull. Continue past another sidepull and follow the slanting crack past pockets, and finish right. Blowing the topout on this problem would be very bad! (V5) (SS TO RBL)

16. **Crash and Burn: Start on a high jug and power past a flake to a sloping rail. Make a difficult move off the sloping rail to the top. A fall at the crux can send you flying off backwards—be sure to have a spotter. This problem has recently seen improvements in the "landing zone." (V5) (SS TO)

    a. *Variation: Adds the sit-start. (V5) (SS TO)

    b. ***Wave Crasher: It's hard to imagine a V3 among all the 4s and 5s! Start on the high jug and power past layaways to a jug. Finish with a dicey topout. (V3) (TO HB BL)

17. *Blood and Guts: Start on a sloping sidepull and edge just right of the low ledge. Move up past an incut flake to good edges.

Power off edges to the top. Finish either straight up or out left (easier). (V4) (SS TO BL)

18. **Cyrax: Big brother to the Gunks classic "Lorax." Start on a hollow pinch and pocket beneath the reverse C. Power past a sloper, a jug, and another sloper, finishing over the top. (V2) (SS TO)

    a. **Variation: Eliminates the sit-start. (V1) (TO)

    b. **Botox: Give the public what they demand! Start on the sloper just above the reverse "C" and throw for the next sloper. Finish over the top. Height dependant. (V3/4) (TO)

    c. *Cortex: Start the same, but at the first sloper, traverse left across the sloping lip

Dan Brayack finds a static way around the throw on *Crash and Burn.* PHOTO BY CARL SAMPLES

Lower Fiddle Area

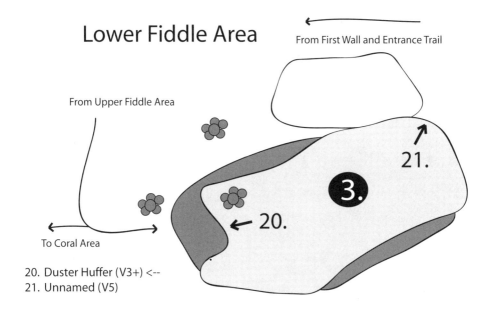

From First Wall and Entrance Trail

From Upper Fiddle Area

21.

3.

← 20.

To Coral Area

20. Duster Huffer (V3+) <--
21. Unnamed (V5)

to a ledge. Continue through jugs and finish left of the sickly tree. (V3) (SS TO)

19. **Butter Face: Start on a low sloper (in front of the small tree) and continue past a jug and slopers to the top. (V1) (SS TO)

Boulder 3:
Lower Fiddle Area

20. ***Duster Huffer: A great power/endurance problem established by *Rock and Ice* editor Jeff Jackson. Start matched on a right-facing slot. Move up and slightly left through incut flakes to a horizontal. Traverse left across edges for about 15 feet and finish up the sloping left arête. To retreat from the top, have your buddy move the pad and jump. (V3+) (TO)

21. **Start on the far left side of the block on nasty slopers. Trend up and right, following the sloping arête past a pocket and pinch to a jug horizontal. Finish at the horn. (V5) (SS TO BL)

Tim Keenan on the powerful *Duster Huffer.*

Coral Area

The Coral Area features a handful of high-quality problems spread out among five boulders. The hike to and from this area can be arduous, but the problems are worth the hike. There are about a dozen low-quality problems in this area. However, the quality of these problems and the approach do not warrant listing in this guide. *Coral* (V7) is one of the most coveted "hard" problems in the forest.

To reach this area, continue on the main trail to the Fiddle Area. Locate the feint trail at the corner of Boulder 2 in the Fiddle Area. Climb over several logs if need be and follow this trail down toward *Duster Huffer*. At the T, make a right and traverse the hillside for about 15 yards. Cut down the hill, aiming to the right of the first large boulder in front of you (Boulder 1).

This area is broken up into the Upper Coral Area (Boulders 1–3) and Lower Coral Area (Boulders 4–5).

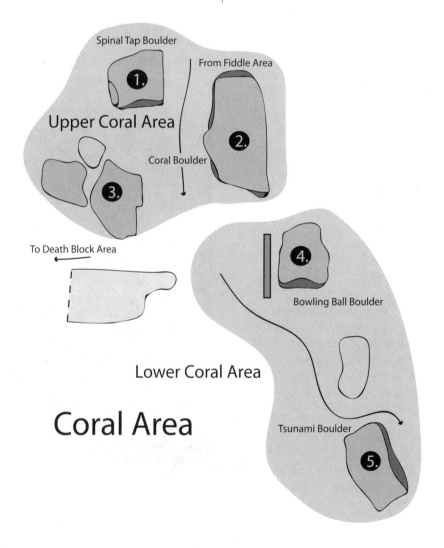

Upper Coral Area

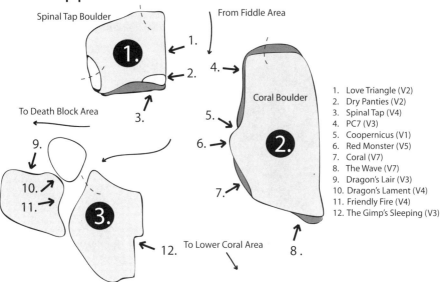

Spinal Tap Boulder

From Fiddle Area

1. 2.

4.

Coral Boulder

To Death Block Area

3. 5.

6.

9.

10. 11.

7.

12. To Lower Coral Area

8.

1. Love Triangle (V2)
2. Dry Panties (V2)
3. Spinal Tap (V4)
4. PC7 (V3)
5. Coopernicus (V1)
6. Red Monster (V5)
7. Coral (V7)
8. The Wave (V7)
9. Dragon's Lair (V3)
10. Dragon's Lament (V4)
11. Friendly Fire (V4)
12. The Gimp's Sleeping (V3)

Boulder 1: Spinal Tap Boulder

The best retreat from the problems on the Spinal Tap Boulder is to continue up the sketchy slab (through the tree) to the easy backside.

1. ★★★Love Triangle: Start right of the low triangle and follow the rising ledge to the second triangle. Step left and finish with a long, frightful move to the top. The topout is straightforward. (V2) (TO SHB RBL)

2. ★★Dry Panties: Start on a high flake and continue past another flake to an edge. Power past an intermediate sloper to the top. (V2) (SS TO BL)

3. ★★Spinal Tap: Local hardman Mike Kelly pulled a block that weighed 18.4 pounds off the top of this problem . . . onto his neck. He survived, hence the name. Start matched on a low incut and move up past a sidepull and pinch to a pocket. Continue up and over the

grim bulge to entertain the harrowing topout moves. (V4) (SS TO)

Boulder 2: Coral Boulder

If you can do the problems on this boulder, the downclimb should be nothing for you, but you probably would not want to send your tubby girlfriend or boyfriend up the backside of this boulder to take pictures! Also, the talus by this boulder has played host to "crash-pad-surfing" contests. Start at the top, run, and jump and see how far you can surf your crash pad down the hill. *(This is a joke! Don't actually do this!)*

4. ★★★PC7: Such a beautiful, proud, over-hanging problem; just pray that the flake doesn't blow! Follow the large left-facing flake through several powerful moves to a jug. Continue up and right past perfect pockets to a horizontal. Be sure to find the "topout" jug a few feet over the top and right. (V3) (TO HB BL)

Dan Brayack hoping nothing blows on PC7.
PHOTO BY TIM WEADON

5. ***Coopernicus: A testament to Carl Sample's visionary highballing and a pun on the famous moon crater. Start on a sidepull and make a subtle move to a jug. Suck it up and make a frightful move up and right past an incut sidepull and pocket to a reasonable topout. (V1) (TO SHB BL)

6. **Red Monster: Start on two opposing flakes and make a long move to a razor edge. Continue through edges to join the small dihedral for the finish. This problem is very sharp. (V5) (HB TO)

7. ****Coral (aka Green Monster): So good! This problem separates the men from the boys. Start inside the hueco on sloping edges. Make long moves through thin edges to a set of pockets. Continue out left past a jug and finish. (V7) (SS TO)

a. *Variation: Start the same, but move right to a sidepull. Make a long move for a round edge and continue to the top. (V5) (SS TO)

8. **The Wave: Ascend desperate overhanging rails to the top. (V7) (TO HB)

Boulder 3

9. *Dragon's Lair: Step up to an edge and make a hard smear move over the bulge. Follow the slab to the top, avoiding both arêtes. (V3) (TO)

10. *Dragon's Lament: A friction-dependent problem. Power through an awkward start on an undercling and continue up the arête past a pinch, to the top. (V4) (SS TO BL)

11. **Friendly Fire: Nothing beats trying to beat a friend to an FA! Though Timmy got it first. . . . Start in the "hole" and follow left-facing flakes up and right past a sidepull to a pocket. Continue with several thin moves over the bulge and finish. Be sure to have a spotter for this problem. (V4) (SS TO BL)

12. **The Gimp's Sleeping: Awkward, but very good! Paw up the arête to a good sidepull. Continue digging to a deep gaston, finishing with a long move to the "Thank God" top. (V3) (TO)

Boulder 4:
Bowling Ball Boulder

13. ***Bowling Ball: Start on two pockets and make a powerful set of moves past grim slopers and pockets to the top. (V4) (TO BL)

14. ***The Shocker: A good, setup throw. Start on the arête on a jug-pocket and high right foot. Hang, get a good swing, and throw up and left to a pocket. Continue to

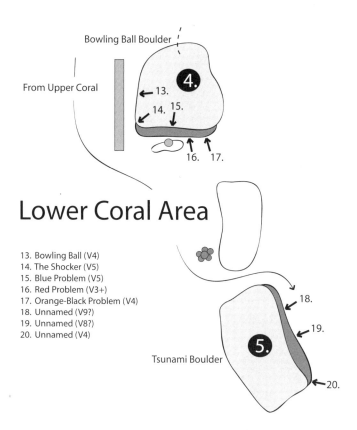

Bowling Ball Boulder

From Upper Coral

4.

13.

14. 15.

16. 17.

Lower Coral Area

13. Bowling Ball (V4)
14. The Shocker (V5)
15. Blue Problem (V5)
16. Red Problem (V3+)
17. Orange-Black Problem (V4)
18. Unnamed (V9?)
19. Unnamed (V8?)
20. Unnamed (V4)

18.

19.

5.

Tsunami Boulder

20.

the top, finishing just right of *Bowling Ball*. (V5) (TO)

The Gym Face

The next set of problems is included for the benefit of all those gym rats out there. These problems are short, powerful, and have grim topouts!

15. **Blue Problem: Start in front of the tree on an edge and sidepull. Move up past a sloper, finishing right through grim slopers. This problem uses feet from the *Red Problem*. Be sure not to brain bash the tree. (V5) (SS TO BL)

  a. **The Punisher: If *The Shocker* just isn't doing it for her, try *The Punisher*. Start as normal, but at the lip, traverse left across your

choice of loose jugs to join *The Shocker*. (V6) (SS TO)

16. **Red Problem: Start 2 feet right of the tree on the ledge. Move up past a razor jug and make a long move through edges, finishing directly over the bulge. (V3+) (SS TO)

17. *Orange-Black Problem: Start on a high pocket and pinch. Move up to two slopers and a pocket. Continue a few feet left and finish with a grim mantel. This problem uses feet from the *Red Problem*. Avoid the right arête. (V4) (SS TO)

Boulder 5: Tsunami Boulder

To reach this boulder, continue down the hill about 50 yards. Walk past a moderately sized boulder and look for the subtle uphill face of this boulder. This boulder features some of the hardest problems in the forest.

18. Rumored to be a David Hume problem. Start on an edge and ascend the desperate face. (V9?) (TO)

19. Another desperate line. (V8?) (TO)

20. ★★Start on a right side of the left arête and follow the pristine rail to the top. (V4) (TO)

Moby's Dick Area

The Moby's Dick Area features a plethora of classic problems. *Moby's Dick* (V3), *Moby's*

Mantel (V4), and *Humility* (V5) are high-quality midrange problems. For the moderate but confident boulderer, the Moby Slab offers a handful of delicate problems. Also, one of the hardest established problems in the forest, the *Razor Arête* (V9), is located in this area.

From the entrance trail, make a right (before Junction 1) and follow the trail past the First Wall (on the right) and the Fiddle Area (on the left) until you see an obvious triangular boulder. This is Boulder 1 of the Moby's Dick Area.

This area is broken into three subareas: Moby's Dick Boulder (Boulder 1), Tier 1 (Boulders 2 and 3), and Tier 2 (Boulder 4).

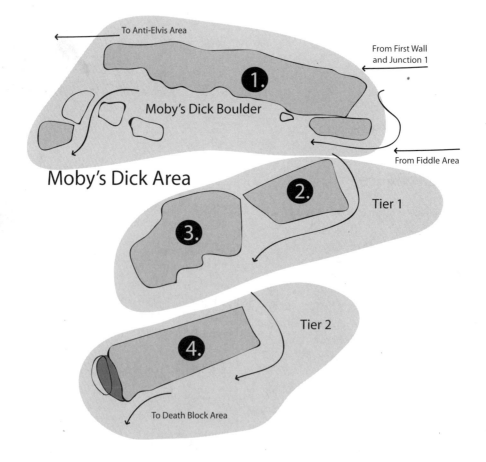

Boulder 1:
Moby's Dick Boulder

1. ***Moby's Mantel (aka the Moby Mantel): Start on a knob and pocket. Avoiding the awkward talus, move right past a gaston and sloper to a sidepull. Continue right, past a pocket to a strenuous mantel. (V4) (SS TO)

a. Start on slopers and traverse left across pockets to join the Mantel problem at the mantel. (V3+/V4) (SS TO)

2. *Sloper Dyno: Start on the sidepull pocket and sloper and throw for the three-finger edge. (V6) (TO)

3. Rumor has it that this has been done. Start on low pockets in the right center of the face. Move out left past desperate sidepulls and a bad pocket to the top. (V?) (TO)

4. ****Moby's Dick (aka Moby's Fin): One of the best of the grade! Definitely a classic for the standard-issue bouldering mongrel. Start low and ascend the overhanging

Tim Keenan throws down on *Sloper Dyno.*

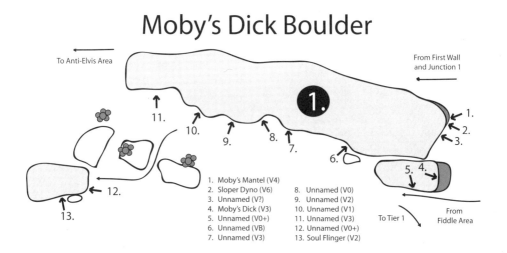

Moby's Dick Boulder

To Anti-Elvis Area

From First Wall
and Junction 1

11.

10.

9.

8.

7.

6.

5. 4.

1.
2.
3.

12.

13.

To Tier 1

From
Fiddle Area

1. Moby's Mantel (V4)
2. Sloper Dyno (V6)
3. Unnamed (V?)
4. Moby's Dick (V3)
5. Unnamed (V0+)
6. Unnamed (VB)
7. Unnamed (V3)

8. Unnamed (V0)
9. Unnamed (V2)
10. Unnamed (V1)
11. Unnamed (V3)
12. Unnamed (V0+)
13. Soul Flinger (V2)

Matt Bosley on the Moby Project.

pinnacle. Finish with a long move to the top. (V3) (SS TO)

Moby Slab

This slab (problems 5 to 11) features a handful of quality foot-intensive moderate problems.

5. ★Start in the center of the detached flake and ascend the low-angle slab to the ledge. (V0+) (TO)

6. Start on the huge, left-facing flake. Continue up the slab, following opposing flakes to the top. (VB) (TO BL)

7. ★★Thin and foot intensive! Start on imaginary edges under the large undercling several feet right of the dirty flake system. Make thin moves on smears to the jug undercling.

Continue up and slightly left, finishing just right of the broken crack. (V3) (TO)

8. ★★Start on a left-facing edge just left of the sickly tree. Follow the left-facing weakness past an incut undercling, through jugs to the top. *Note:* This problem is a good downclimb. (V0) (TO)

9. ★★Start just right of the small cave and move past an undercling and thin left-facing flakes to the top. (V2) (TO)

10. ★Start about 5 feet left of the large tree on a jug and ascend immaculate left-facing flakes to the top. (V1) (TO)
    a. ★★Variation: Start on the same jug, but mantel. Continue left through good holds to the top. (V0+) (TO)

11. ★★Start just right of the flat talus on an edge and sidepull. Engage thin moves up and slightly right, avoiding the left "arête" until the top. (V3) (TO)

To reach the next boulder, travel about 10 yards through several boulders.

12. ★Pleasant moves on bullet rock; too bad it's not longer. Start on the left side of the arête on an edge and follow the left side of the arête to the top. (V0+) (TO)
    a. Variation: Layback the overhanging right side of the arête to the top. (V3) (TO)

13. ★★Soul Flinger: Characterized by thin, balancey moves on bad holds. Start just left of the flat talus on a pinch and follow thin edges up and slightly left to the top. (V2) (TO)

Tier 1: Boulders 2 and 3

Boulder 2

To reach the next set of boulders, continue down the hill from the Moby's Dick Boulder.
    Problems 14 to 17 are great core-intensive

Moby's Dick Area: Tier 1

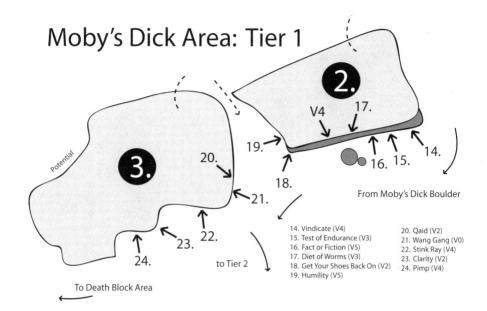

From Moby's Dick Boulder

14. Vindicate (V4)
15. Test of Endurance (V3)
16. Fact or Fiction (V5)
17. Diet of Worms (V3)
18. Get Your Shoes Back On (V2)
19. Humility (V5)

20. Qaid (V2)
21. Wang Gang (V0)
22. Stink Ray (V4)
23. Clarity (V2)
24. Pimp (V4)

to Tier 2

To Death Block Area

problems; however, the holds are all questionable. Let's all just hope that no key holds break! Be sure to scope topout holds prior to trying these problems.

14. **Vindicate: Surprisingly good! Start on a deep flake and pinch. Move up and slightly right past sharp flakes to an undercling. Make a long move off the undercling past edges to an entertaining topout. Just hope that no "tubbies" are strong enough to make it to the upper holds. (V4) (SS TO)
  a. Eliminates the sit-start. (V3) (TO)

15. **Test of Endurance: Start on an undercling and move past an incut flake to a suspect jug. Power off jug past a gaston to a jug. (V3) (HB TO)

16. **Fact or Fiction: Characterized by long reaches, bad holds, and nonexistent feet, but not all at the same time! Establish on the large jug and make a powerful mantel to an undercling (long reach). Continue up and right past a sloping edge (bad holds) to a right-facing sidepull. Make a long move for a jug (nonex-

istent feet) and finish. (V5) (TO HB)

17. **Diet of Worms: Start just right of the twin trees on a ledge. Move up past an edge to an undercling. Continue past a right-facing flake to a sloper and entertain the hairball topout on edges and a sloper. (V3) (TO)

18. **Get Your Shoes Back On: Harder until some jerk-face removed the tree. Don't cut trees down! Start on pocket pinch and edge. Ascend the arête past pockets and edges to the top. (V2) (SS TO)

19. ***Humility: Start just left of the arête on a good finger lock. Step up to an awkward pocket and continue up and right past pockets and a gaston, finishing on the sloping horn 2 feet left of the arête. This problem uses feet on the arête. (V5) (TO)

Boulder 3

20. *Qaid: Great rock and good moves—too bad it's not longer. Start on the deep jug pocket and undercling. Move past another

Bob Rentka takes off his human mask for *Qaid*.

pocket to a sidepull. Continue past a horizontal, a pocket, and an edge to the top. This problem avoids holds out left. (V2) (SS TO)

a. **Variation: Eliminates the sit-start. Start on sidepull pockets and continue as normal. (V1) (TO)

21. **Wang Gang: Though not independent, this problem is a good moderate. Start just left of the previous problem (high jug foot) on a left-facing flake and shared pocket. Move directly up past a horizontal and pocket to the top. (V0) (TO)

22. Stink Ray: Start on an undercling and make a long move past an edge to the top. (V4) (TO)

23. **Clarity: Start on opposing edges. Power back right to the large flake and continue up past an edge to the top. (V2) (SS TO)

a. **Variation: Eliminates the back flake and uses a sidepull/undercling on the small roof instead. (V3) (SS TO)

24. *Pimp: Start on high edge and a sidepull. Pimp through left-facing edges to the top. (V4) (SS TO)

Tier 2: Boulder 4

25. FUP: Start on a questionable right-facing edge and jug. Move out right to a pinch and engage the slopey topout. (V3) (TO)

26. ***Special Needs: Start on two opposing sidepulls. Make a long move to a sloping edge and continue past a thin edge, making a powerful move for a jug. This problem has good moves but is a little sharp. (V3+) (TO)

27. Hollow Scary: Start on a pinch and left-facing edge. Move up past a left-facing flake

Moby's Dick Area: Tier 2

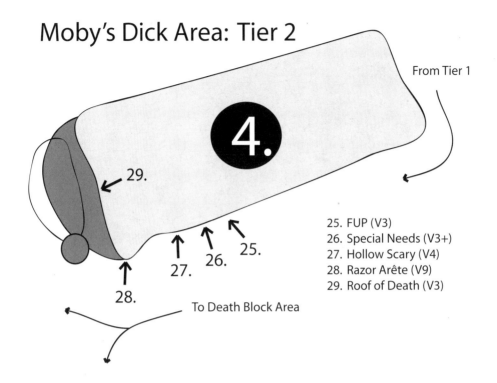

From Tier 1

4.

29.

27. 26. 25.

28.

To Death Block Area

25. FUP (V3)
26. Special Needs (V3+)
27. Hollow Scary (V4)
28. Razor Arête (V9)
29. Roof of Death (V3)

to a left-facing edge. Continue through hollow scary flakes to the top. (V4) (SS TO)

28. ****Razor Arête (aka Butterfly Arête): A Brian Janaszek–Joel Brady masterpiece! Such a beautiful yet hard line. Start on a pinch and edge and follow grim edges and pockets to the top. (V9) (SS TO HB)

 a. ****Variation: Eliminates the sit-start. (V6) (TO HB)

29. ***Roof of Death (aka ROD): Unless you like big moves with a really bad landing, this problem probably isn't for you. Start on a left-facing flake and move up past a horizontal to a knob. Suck it up and make several big, powerful moves through "jugs" and stick the top. Be sure to have a few spotters and at least four pads. (V3) (TO RBL)

Death Block Area

The Death Block area boasts a bounty of high-quality and difficult problems. *Death Block* (V6) is one of the most sought-after problems in the forest. Also, the abnormally popular *The Allusionist* (V7) has caught some serious hype. There are a handful of good midrange problems in this area such as *Proana* (V4), *Exorexic* (V3), and *Given to Fly* (V2). Finally, the Death Block Area is home to the hardest "graded" problem in forest: *Heel Clacker* (V10), which was established by Pittsburgh climber Joel Brady. *Note:* The problem now universally known as *Death Block* and the companion right arête have been know as "Slash and Burn" in the past.

 Though a semiarduous approach, the walk is certainly worth it! Continue past Tier 2 of the Moby's Dick Area on the trail that cuts directly down the hill. You will see a

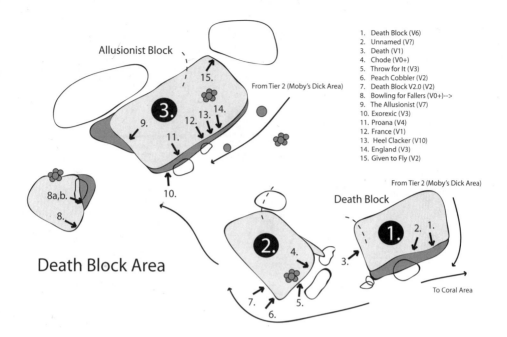

Allusionist Block

From Tier 2 (Moby's Dick Area)

1. Death Block (V6)
2. Unnamed (V?)
3. Death (V1)
4. Chode (V0+)
5. Throw for It (V3)
6. Peach Cobbler (V2)
7. Death Block V2.0 (V2)
8. Bowling for Fallers (V0+)-->
9. The Allusionist (V7)
10. Exorexic (V3)
11. Proana (V4)
12. France (V1)
13. Heel Clacker (V10)
14. England (V3)
15. Given to Fly (V2)

From Tier 2 (Moby's Dick Area)

Death Block

Death Block Area

To Coral Area

boulder with an obvious crack in the back. This is the *Death Block* (Boulder 1). Boulder 3 can also be reached from Tier 2 in the Moby's Dick Area.

Boulder 1: Death Block

1. ****Death Block: A great problem! One of the best at the grade in the forest, characterized by the huge, precariously pasted "Death Block." Start on edges and continue up the beautifully featured overhanging face to the Death Block. Finish with an easy move over the top. This problem is reach dependant. (V6) (SS TO HB)

 a. ***Variation: Eliminates the sit-start. (V4) (TO HB)

2. Start on an undercling and follow the obvious left-facing flake to the top. At press time this problem has not received a confirmed ascent. (V?) (TO HB RBL)

3. *Death: Not as good as the cereal, but just as crunchy. A pun on the popular cereal "Life." Start on a large pocket and move up past a horizontal to a sloper. Finish over the top. (V1) (TO)

Boulder 2

4. **Chode: Wider than it is long. Start on the right side of the boulder on opposing sidepulls. Move up through pleasant pockets, finishing over the right arête. (V0+) (TO)

5. **Throw for It: Start in the center of the face under the sickly tree on cannon-ball jugs. Setup on pockets and throw for a sloper to the right of the tree. Finish matched on the top lip and jump. This problem avoids topping out because doing so would necessitate killing the tree. (V3) (BL)

6. **Peach Cobbler: So sweet! Start on the left side of the arête, climbing between the arête and a vertical jug. Scum your way up the left side of the arête using compression moves, finishing through fractured, yet thankfully solid, jugs. (V2) (TO HB)

7. *Death Block V2.0: Start about 5 feet left of the arête on an undercling and sharp right-facing sidepull. Using a shared foot, move up past a pocket and edges to a huge, hollow-sounding block. Finish with a subtle hop onto the top of the block. (V2) (TO HB)

Boulder 3:
The Allusionist Block

To reach The Allusionist Block, trend up and left from the previous boulder. This boulder is the obvious overhanging block up the hill. This boulder can also be reached by trending down and right from Tier 2 in the Moby's Dick Area.

8. **Bowling for Fallers: Start on a large pocket on the left side of the narrow face. Connect the three big pockets and finish by stepping right, past a horizontal to the top. (V0+) (TO)

    a. **Gutter Ball: Start on a jug and sidepull several feet right of the third pocket. Continue up the prow past pockets and vertical jugs to the top. The detached block is on. (V0+) (TO)

    b. **Seven-Ten Split: Start the same as Gutter Ball, but power out left to pocket 3. Finish right as per the normal variation. This problem avoids the detached rock. (V2) (TO BL)

9. ***The Allusionist: Big moves between bad holds on an overhanging face. This problem has been catching some serious hype! Start in the broken crack and move up and left, ascending the desperate nose to the top. (V7) (TO HB)

10. ***Exorexic: This short little power

Kevin Shon lining up for the *Seven-Ten Split*.

problem is sure to get you fired up! Start on a left-facing flake and power up and right to a right-facing flake. Continue past a pocket to a very frictional topout. (V3) (SS TO)

11. ***Proana: Start on the sloping ledge in front of the "UFO" talus. Move up and left past a sloper and then power back right, following incut jugs to the top. (V4) (SS TO)

12. *France: Not really worth the trouble unless you're liberating England. Start on a high sidepull and edge. Make a long move to a dark jug. Continue up and right and then finish back left with a grungy topout. (V1) (SS TO)

13. **Heel Clacker: A Joel Brady test piece. Start just right of *France* on a desperate sidepull and edge. Power past a square-cut, sloping edge to a relatively good sidepull. Finish with a mantel. (V10?) (SS TO)

14. **England: Start on two edges and a high left foot. Power to the lip, finishing through grim edges and slopers. (V3) (TO)

15. ***Given to Fly: Start on a pocket and undercling and slap up the immaculate prow, finishing over the point. (V2) (TO BL)
   a. *Given to Suck: Impeccable stone, but not impeccable moves. Start in the center of the face on opposing edges. Continue up and left, following the crack to the top. (V1) (TO)

Anti-Elvis Area

The Anti-Elvis Area features the power-oriented classic *Anti-Elvis* (V4) and its easier companion, *Elvis Legs* (V3).

To reach this area, continue past the Moby's Dick Area along the main trail for about 100 feet until you reach an obvious fork. Trend left, aiming for the large triangular block. Cut through the chasm to reach this area. This area is quite popular: If you do not see chalk, you are probably in the wrong place.

Boulder 1

This boulder features a "3-foot-high" lip traverse. It seems to be a continuing theme at Coopers Rock.

**1. ***Start on the right side of the roof on two pockets. Traverse left across the lip past a pocket and edges to a jug on the nose. Finish over the nose. (V4) (SS TO)

Boulder 2:
Anti-Elvis Boulder

2. ****Anti-Elvis: Start on an edge on the arête and your choice of slopers. Make a power, yet surprisingly easy, move to a perfect sloper. Power off the sloper to a pinch and make a long move to the lip. Make several intense "heartbreaker" moves over the lip to a jug. Follow the slab up and left to the top. (V4) (SS TO)
   a. **Variation: Start as described above, but match on the perfect sloper. Move left through a pinch and flat edge, making a hard move to lip. Finish over the slab. (V5) (SS TO)

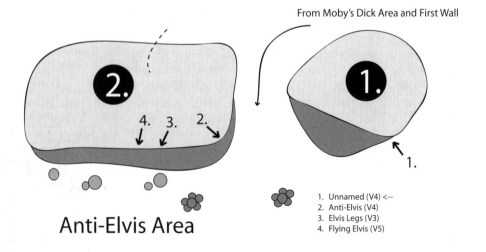

From Moby's Dick Area and First Wall

Anti-Elvis Area

1. Unnamed (V4) <--
2. Anti-Elvis (V4)
3. Elvis Legs (V3)
4. Flying Elvis (V5)

3. ***Elvis Legs: A really good, powerful moderate. Start in front of the tree on a jug. Traverse low right through jugs (low feet are on) and a flake. Make a big move to a blind right-facing edge. Continue up and left past a jug, finishing to the right of the rhododendron. (V3) (SS TO)

4. **Flying Elvis: If you like big throws and don't care about blowing out your shoulder when you're thirty, this is the problem for you! Start on a jug and make a ridiculous throw for the lip. Finish over the top. Grade is dependant on height and body type. (V5) (TO)

The Egg

Farther past the Anti-Elvis Area is The Egg. This boulder is at about the same level as *Death Block*. There are a handful of high-quality difficult and moderate problems. Further details in regard to this boulder were left out to allow boulderers to retain and reserve the "combat ascent" or "virgin on-sight."

In-between Area

There are a handful of high-quality problems interspersed between the Tilted Tree and Roadside Areas. Go out and explore!

ROADSIDE ROCKS

Directions: From the entrance gate, follow the main road for 2.5 miles until you reach a large parking lot. Park on the left, near the kiosk. Be sure to sign in at the kiosk and follow the established trail down and left. You will walk down a set of stone steps. When you reach the second set of stone steps, continue left for the majority of the problems or veer right for the Warm-up Boulders.

Roadside Rocks truly is the gem of bouldering at Coopers Rock. Because of its easy access, high concentration of quality problems in all ranges, and striking variety of problems, this area has historically been the most popular bouldering area in Coopers Rock State Forest. Problems such as *Woody's Arête* (V3), the *Mad Butcher Traverse* (V2/3), and the *Green Block Test Piece* (V5) are classics. The bouldering overview map shows the first and main portion of the Roadside Area. The Jimi Cliff and Bitch Slap Areas are not shown on this map, but are located further down the trail.

Warm-up Boulders

The Warm-up Boulders feature a multitude of moderate, high-angle slab problems, as well as several intense problems. The classics *Bizzaro* (V5) and *Helicopter* (V5) should not be missed. This is a good area to bring a beginner, especially Boulder 3.

To reach this area, make a sharp right after a large stone step. The main boulder will be directly in front of you.

Roadside Rocks

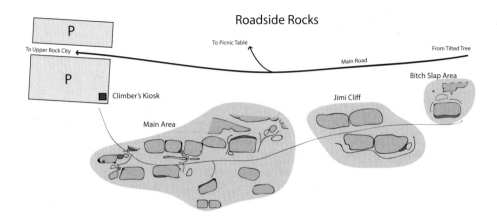

Roadside Rocks

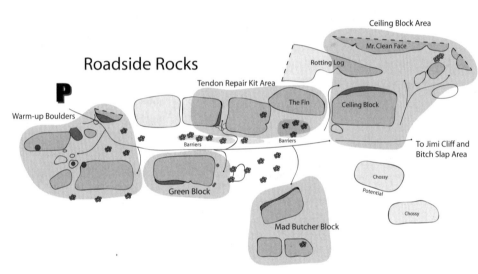

Warm-up Boulders

1. Helicopter (V5)
2. Bizzaro (V5)
3. Apples (V1)
4. Vitamin P (V2)
5. Warm-up Arête (V4)
6. Teen Spirit (V1)
7. Schwang (V0+)
8. Blang (V0)
9. Warm-up Traverse (V0+) -->
10. Unnamed (V0)
11. Unnamed (V0)
12. Unnamed (V0+)
13. Unnamed (VB)
14. Unnamed (V0+)
15. Unnamed (V0)
16. Unnamed (V0)
17. Unnamed (V0)
18. Unnamed (V1)
19. Unnamed (V0+)
20. No Scope (V2)
21. You Got Stuck (V2)
22. Kaleidoscope (V2)
23. Censor (V3)

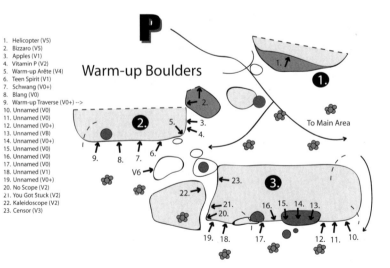

Vicky Arthur taking a ride on *Helicopter.*

Boulder 1: Helicopter

1. ***Helicopter: This "hidden" problem is amazingly long! Start in the back of the cave on a jug. Move out the line of jugs to lip. Pull the lip and continue past a horizontal to the top. (V5) (SS TO)

Boulder 2: Warm-up Boulder

2. ****Bizzaro: Start just outside the cave on a pinch and incut edge. Slap out the "refrigerator" roof using compression strength and heel hooks. Make a long move at the lip and follow the arête to the top. Using a foot from the main boulder is acceptable style. (V5) (SS TO)

   a. *Variation: Start the same, but make a difficult lip move and ascend the left side of the slab on thin edges, avoiding the right arête. (V5) (SS TO)

3. *Apples: Start 2 feet left of the small tree and follow the short line of pockets and edges to the top. (V1) (TO)

4. **Vitamin P: Start 2 feet right of the arête and continue past thin edges and a pocket to the top. (V2) (TO)

5. **Warm-up Boulder Arête: Start on a jug and make short but hard moves through edges and a sidepull to a good edge. Follow the arête over the bulge to the top. You may lose some skin on this one. (V4) (SS TO)

   a. **Variation: Eliminates the sit-start. (V2) (TO)

6. **Teen Spirit: Start on the jug just left of the protruding rock and continue up past a sloping jug, through pleasant horizontals and a pocket to the top. (V1) (SS TO)

7. **Schwang: Start on a horizontal and step up to a jug. Follow the left-facing edges through pockets to the top. (V0+) (TO)

Mike Kelly squeezing juice on *Bizzaro*.

a. **Thwang: A great little dyno! From the jug, throw for and double hand the top. (V1) (TO)

8. *Blang: Start just right of the tree and move past pockets and edges to the top. (V0) (TO)

a. *Lip Traverse: Do *Blang* to the lip and traverse right, finishing at the arête. (V0) (TO)

9. *Warm-up Traverse: Start to the left of the big fir tree and traverse slightly up and right, following the path of least resistance. Finish up the arête. (V0+) (TO HB)

Boulder 3: Beginner's Face

I've always preached that difficulty and quality are not mutually exclusive. The Beginner's Face features a cluster of really easy but quality problems. The Beginner's Face is an excellent destination to kick back and get some mileage or to bring a first-time climber. Many of the problems feature positive holds but technical movements. The problems on this face are really enjoyable. There are a multitude of holds: One can play "choose your own adventure" on the entire face.

10. *Start just left of the arête on a pocket and horizontal. Move up past pockets and edges to the top. (V0) (TO)

11. *Start on a pinch and pocket 2 feet right of protruding point. Continue past a pocket and edge to a long move for the top. (V0) (TO)

12. *Start standing on the protruded point and move up and right past a horizontal to the top. (V0+) (TO)

13. *Start under the right side of the small roof and follow horizontals to the top. (VB) (TO)

14. ★Start under the center of the small roof on thin pockets. Continue up past horizontals and make a frightful topout over the roof. (V0+) (TO HB)

15. ★Start in front of the large tree on pockets. Make a thin move and continue through horizontals, finishing just left of the roof. (V0) (TO)

16. ★A little squeezed. Start on a ledge and right-facing sidepull about 3 feet left of the large tree. Continue up and slightly right past a large pocket, through more pockets to the top. (V0) (TO)

17. ★Also a little squeezed. Step up to a horizontal just right of the rising ledge system. Smear up, past pockets to the top. (V0) (TO)

If you've scored all the previous problems and think that your poop doesn't stink, try the next two problems.

18. ★★Start on a large edge on the right side of the tall, proud face. Move up past horizontals and a right-facing sidepull, through benign pockets to the top. (V1) (TO HB)

19. ★★Start on a pocket and step up to a horizontal. Follow pockets past horizontals, finishing just right of the arête. (V0+) (TO)

20. ★★**No Scope:** Start on a low incut edge on the right side of the arête. Move up and left past edges and a pocket to a ledge. Finish up the arête. (V2) (SS TO HB BL)

21. ★★**You Got Stuck:** A brilliant line! Start on a jug and continue up past a sloping ledge to thin pockets. Make several committing moves up the gently overhanging prow to the top. (V2) (SS TO HB RBL)

22. ★★**Kaleidoscope:** Start on a right-facing sidepull and upgrade, finishing with a big move to the top. (V2) (SS TO)

Be sure to scope the topout and have a spotter for the next problem. There is a low-quality, hard problem on the left corner. However, it is not worth more than a mention.

23. ★**Censor:** If you chalk it, they will come. Start on a horizontal and step up to a jug flake. Continue through edges, past a high pocket to the top. (V3) (HB TO BL)

Green Block

The Green Block has a host of high-quality moderate highball problems, as well as one of the best hard problems in the forest, the

Green Block

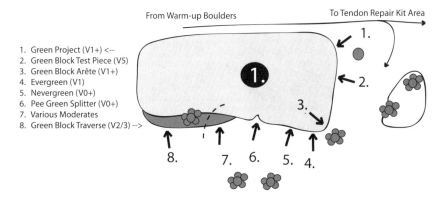

From Warm-up Boulders   To Tendon Repair Kit Area

1. Green Project (V1+) <--
2. Green Block Test Piece (V5)
3. Green Block Arête (V1+)
4. Evergreen (V1)
5. Nevergreen (V0+)
6. Pee Green Splitter (V0+)
7. Various Moderates
8. Green Block Traverse (V2/3) -->

Green Block Test Piece (V5). Though a lot of the moderates on this block are quite high, and the falls would be ugly, the moves up high tend to be moderate and the topouts straightforward. But be careful nonetheless.

To reach the Green Block, continue down the main trail from the second set of stone steps for about 30 yards. The *Green Block Test Piece* is the distinguishing, proud, clean line up the right center of the face. Veer right at the second gap to spot this problem.

Boulder 1: Green Block

1. *Green Project: Start on the right arête near the trail. Traverse left following the horizontal line of jugs. Finish on the same jug as the *Green Block Test Piece*. This is a good

Tall guy Tim Keenan on *Green Block Test Piece*.

problem to clean the "holds" on the *Test Piece*. (V1+)

2. ****Green Block Test Piece: One of the hardest problems in the forest to wire. Holding the crux pocket is desperate; and when it goes, it always somehow feels "easy," where as the rest of the time it just feels impossible. Start on an undercling jug and move up to a really bad pocket. Make a hard move off the pocket and intermediate "edge" to the jug. Classically sandbagged at V4, this has been upgraded based on popular consensus. Condition dependent. (V5)

   a. **Variation 1: Using the opening jug, step up and throw for the finishing jug. If dynoing is your thing, this is a good way to cheat the whole problem. (V5)

   b. Variation 2: Adds the sit-start. (V5) (SS)

   c. *Morning Stroller: Start on the same jug as the Green Block Test Piece, but traverse left, making several powerful reachy pocket moves to a jug. Continue left and finish up the arête. (V3) (HB BL)

3. **Green Block Arête: Start on the right side of the arête on a sidepull and a high pocket (on the arête). Continue past pockets and horizontals to a jug and the top. Landing on the tree would be very bad. (V1+) (HB BL TO)

   a. Variation: Adds the sit-start. Start on the horizontal just right of the arête and continue as described above. (V3) (SS HB BL TO)

4. **Evergreen: Start just left of the arête on a seam and a palm on the arête. Continue up and slightly left through horizontals to a jug under a small roof. Make several precarious moves to the top. The upper moves are a little unnerving and a fall would likely result in a carry-out. Other than that, this is a great problem! (V1) (HB TO)

5. ***Nevergreen: A great moderate! Start on a sloper and seam about 7 feet left of the arête. Move up and left through several jugs and then trend back right to a jug under the small roof. Step right and to a shared finish with the previous problem. Ditto the warning from the previous problem. (V0+) (TO HB)

6. **Pee Green Splitter: Jam the beautiful crack through jugs and a vertical seam to the top. (V0+) (TO HB)

a. *Green Envy: An interesting eliminate that avoids crack. Start just right of the crack on an edge and heinous sloper. Power up the face past a jug and vertical seam to the top. (V2+) (TO HB)

7. There is a plethora of short moderate problems around the no. 7 marker.

8. *Green Block Traverse: Start on the left arête and traverse low, following foot jugs to the Green Block Arête. Finish up the Green Block Arête. Reach dependant. (V2/3) (HB BL)

Tendon Repair Kit Area

Across the trail from the Green Block is the start of the Tendon Repair Kit Area. This area consists of the three large boulders on the left side of the trail. The bold *Mountaineer's Route* (V5), the hidden *Cave Problem* (V3), and the *Tendon Repair Kit* (V3) are must-do problems.

To reach this area, continue down the main trail for about 40 yards.

Boulder 1

1. Just Plain Lazy: Start on the left arête and traverse right on jugs, avoiding the tree at the start. Continue across the face until you reach the break in the boulders. (V0)

To reach the *Cave Problem,* travel through the narrow passageway between the two blocks. You can also walk all the way around The Fin for a longer, but less arduous, approach.

2. ***Cave Problem: A very dynamic, high-quality problem, this hidden gem stays cool in the summer and is protected from precipitation. Start low on jugs and move up and left and then back right, making long powerful moves up the gently overhanging face. Make a wild move to a jug and then another big move, finishing on a jug below the roof of the cave. (V3)

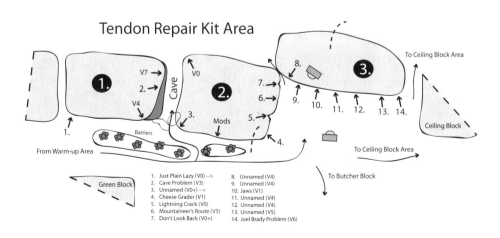

Tendon Repair Kit Area

1. Just Plain Lazy (V0) -->
2. Cave Problem (V3)
3. Unnamed (V0+) -->
4. Cheese Grader (V1)
5. Lightning Crack (V0)
6. Mountaineer's Route (V5)
7. Don't Look Back (V0+)
8. Unnamed (V4)
9. Unnamed (V4)
10. Jaws (V1)
11. Unnamed (V4)
12. Unnamed (V4)
13. Unnamed (V5)
14. Joel Brady Problem (V6)

3. *Start on the arête and traverse right along the horizontal jug. Finish on the off-width crack. (V0+)

Boulder 2:
Tendon Repair Kit

There are a number of moderate boulder problems along the front face that are not worth more than a mention.

To view the topography for problems 4 through 7a, see the topo below.

4. Cheese Grader: Start on the left arête and follow the sloping left arête to the top. (V1) (TO HB)

5. **Lightning Crack: Follow the obvious hand crack up and right to the top. (V0) (TO HB)

a. ***Lightning Bolt: Start just right of the crack on two large pockets. Make a long move to a jug and continue past a high directional pocket to the top. This problem

eliminates the crack and is quite good. *Note:* Many boulders end this problem on the jug halfway up (V3). (V4) (TO HB)

b. ***Tendon Repair Kit: Ascend the crack to the jug and traverse right, past pockets and edges. Finish up or down Don't Look Back. (V3) (TO HB BL)

6. ****Mountaineer's Route Direct: Originally toproped, bouldering is now the standard-issue style for this problem. Start in the center of the face on good pockets. Move up past a grapefruit-size sloper to a jug. Continue past several pockets to a big move for a sloping edge. Make a thought-provoking but easy move to an often dirty top and finish left. This problem is high but has a good flat landing. Don't throw for the top. (V5) (TO HB)

a. ****Mountaineer's Route Original: Start as described above, but from the jug, move up and right past a line of pockets to a vertical pocket. Move back left through several slopers and continue straight up to fin-

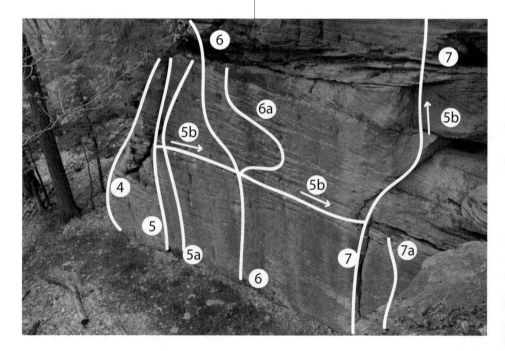

Bob Value on the *Mountaineer's Route.*
PHOTO FROM THE SITH COLLLECTION

ish. This was the original line of ascent. (V5) (TO HB BL)

7. *Don't Look Back:* Ascend the striking crack to the ledge. Continue up the crack and face to the top. (V0+) (TO HB BL)

    a. *Variation:* Start just right of the crack on a pocket and pinch and follow pockets to the jug. (V5) (SS)

Boulder 3: The Fin

This boulder is characterized by scary, highball topouts with bad landings. If it weren't for the topouts, these problems would be some of the best moderates in the forest. The topouts on all of these problems are not recommended.

    To view the topography for problems 8 through 14, see the topo below.

8. Start just right of the crevice on a left-facing sidepull. Follow often wet, often mossy slopers and jug to the ledge. The topout is not recommended. (V4) (SS)

9. ★★Start about 10 feet right of the small cave on an angling edge. Power up past slopers, out right to an undercling. Continue back left past a sloping edge to a good pinch. Make a long move to finish on the "bowling ball" sloper. (V4) (SS)

10. ★Jaws: Start on an incut jug and move up through sloping jugs and an undercling. Finish by tagging the top and then downclimb the problem. Don't bother with the topout, it's hard and is total death if you blow it. (V1) (HB BL)

11. ★★Start on a large flake and continue past an incut pocket and undercling to a good but thin jug. Trend up and right through aesthetic moves, aiming for an incut edge a foot right of the secondary ledge system. It is advisable to walk around and tick this edge. The topout is the crux. (V4) (TO SHB BL)

a. ★★Variation start: Start on the right-facing flake 3 feet right of the normal start (problem 12) and move left to join problem 11 at the undercling. (V4) (TO SHB BL)

12. ★Start on the right-facing flake 3 feet right of the normal start. Continue straight up and slightly right past a divot to a sloper (V3). Move left on the horizontal to join the topout of the previous problem. (V4) (TO SHB BL)

13. ★★Start a few feet left of the right arête on a sidepull. Move up and right past sidepulls and slopers to a sloping rail. Power off the sloping rail (V4) past a pocket to a harrowing topout. (V5) (TO SHB RBL)

14. ★Joel Brady Problem: Ascend the blunt arête, making a desperate move for the top. Suck it up and finish with a hairball mantel. *Note:* This problem uses a layaway from the previous problem. If you value your life, you may want to avoid this one! (V6) (TO HB BL)

The Mad Butcher Block

The Mad Butcher Block is home to the classic *Mad Butcher Traverse* (V2/3), as well as a handful of mostly moderate, high-quality problems. This block is distinguished by the line of chalk about 5 feet off the ground and is caped by a small roof. The block is about 15 to 20 feet tall; however, most problems just end at the upper roof band. The problems are graded in accordance to this finish. If one chooses to topout, the most convenient downclimb is the back right arête, which is about 30 feet tall but moderate.

As you continue past the Green Block, the next distinguishing block on your right is the Mad Butcher Block. The next boulder down the hill (Second Half) has a low-quality problem and variation.

Climbing up The Fin. PHOTO BY CARL SAMPLES

The Mad Butcher Block

From Tendon Repair Kit Area

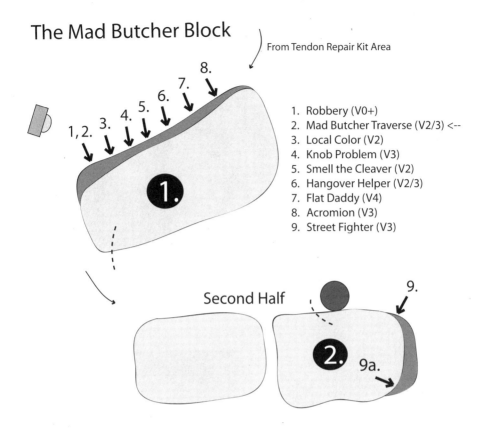

1. Robbery (V0+)
2. Mad Butcher Traverse (V2/3) <--
3. Local Color (V2)
4. Knob Problem (V3)
5. Smell the Cleaver (V2)
6. Hangover Helper (V2/3)
7. Flat Daddy (V4)
8. Acromion (V3)
9. Street Fighter (V3)

Second Half

Boulder 1: Mad Butcher Block

For the first six problems, the best line of descent is to traverse right and downclimb *Robbery* (bad landing), or just downclimb the problem.

To view the topography for problems 1 through 8, see the topo on p. 56.

1. **Robbery: Start just left of the prominent arête on a jug. Move up and left through the line of jugs, finishing on a jug below the crack. This is a good moderate roof problem. (V0+) (BL)

    a. *I Got Robbed: A fun variation. Start on the same jug, but make a long move to a sloper about 3 feet right of the normal finish. (V1) (BL)

2. ****Mad Butcher Traverse: Start on *Robbery* and follow the horizontal line left, through increasingly difficult moves, to the left end of the block. Stand on the ledge to finish. Reach dependent. (V2/3)

3. ***Local Color: A great chic problem. Start in front of the last protruding rock on a good letter box and sloper. Make a long move for an edge below the roof. Move off this edge up and right to the finish on *Robbery.* (V2)

    a. **Throwing Local: A more manly approach to the subtle *Local Color.* From the

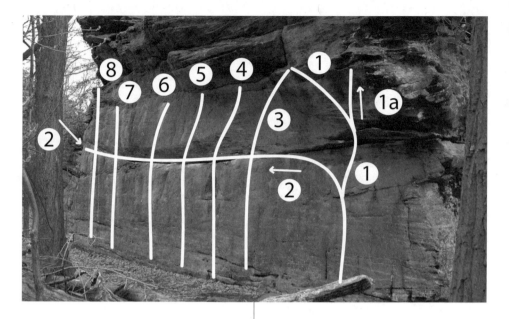

starting letterbox, throw up and right to the finishing jug. (V2)

4. **Knob Problem: Start in a good horizontal and move up past a right-facing knob. Finish on the horizontal band below the roof. (V3)

5. **Smell the Cleaver: Start on the horizontal just right of the tree and continue past a seam to the line of pockets. (V2)

6. ***Hangover Helper: Start on the horizontal just left of the tree. Engage a powerful press move and finish on the obvious but deceptive edge. Super-sneaky trick beta makes this problem much easier. (V2/3)

For the next two problems, the best line of descent is to traverse left to the arête and downclimb.

7. ***Flat Daddy: Start on the left-slanting jug and continue past a good edge to a heinous sloping edge. Make a powerful move off the sloping edge up and right past the blank face to a sloper. Condition dependant. (V4)

Dan Brayack recovering on *Hangover Helper.*

8. *Acromion: Start 3 feet right of the arête on two seams. Move up, past a sloping rail to a jug. (V3)

Boulder 2: Second Half

This boulder is located directly behind the Mad Butcher Block. It has one problem with two variations. The following information was provided by Mike Flack.

9. *Street Fighter: Start on a left-facing flake and right pocket. Move up and right past pockets and a jug, through sidepulls to the ledge. (V3) (SS)

   a. Variation: Start on the left arête and traverse right across jugs and slopers to join Street Fighter at midheight. (V3)

Ceiling Block Area

The Ceiling Block Area features a handful of high-quality problems as well as many good toproping routes. This area is often targeted for guide and newbie traffic, so you may want to consider a different area during peak usage hours. This area features the classic *Woody's Arête* (V3) and the super-hard *The Hammer* (V7), as well as several other high-quality difficult problems.

To reach this area, continue down the main trail past the Tendon Repair Kit Area.

Boulder 1: Ceiling Block

1. ***The Hammer (aka Perkuno's Hammer): This heinous and long-standing project was finally sent by local hard man John Sirios. Start on the vertical seam. Move past pockets and a thin seam to a sloper. Finish on the jug and jump. (V7)

2. ***Ain't No Leaner: Start on the right side of the arête on a sidepull pocket and palm on the arête. Paw up the right side of the arête past a sloping edge to a blind edge on the arête. Finish on the jug. (V3)

3. ***Extramundane: Step off the small boulder with your left hand on a sloping edge and your right on the undercling-pinch

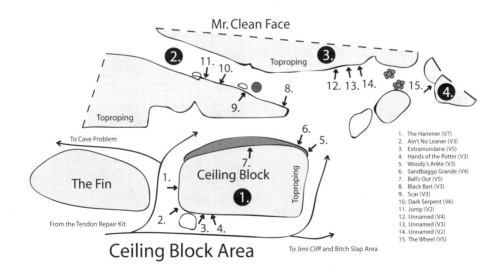

Ceiling Block Area

1. The Hammer (V7)
2. Ain't No Leaner (V3)
3. Extramundane (V5)
4. Hands of the Potter (V3)
5. Woody's Arête (V3)
6. Sandbaggo Grande (V4)
7. Ball's Out (V5)
8. Black Bart (V3)
9. Scar (V3)
10. Dark Serpent (V6)
11. Jump (V2)
12. Unnamed (V4)
13. Unnamed (V3)
14. Unnamed (V2)
15. The Wheel (V5)

Bob Rentka on his weekly Saturday stroll up *The Hammer*.

up and slightly right through slopers and an undercling to a set of jugs. Either finish on the jugs or on the sloping ledge. (V2)

5. ****Woody's Arête (aka Bastard's Edge): One of the best problems in the forest! Start on a sloper and edge and ascend the striking arête to the upper horizontal. Hump it! (V3)

    a. ***Variation: Adds the sit-start. This variation is quite sharp. (V5) (SS)

6. **Sandbaggo Grande: Start a few feet right of the arête on opposing edges. Follow balancey moves through thin edges to a jug under the roof. Either downclimb the problem or traverse left and downclimb Woody's Arête (pad accordingly). (V4) (HB)

pocket. Solve the puzzle and end on the jug. Extremely tall climbers may find this problem "soft." (V5)

    a. **Variation 1: Start off the ground on the undercling and continue as described above. (V6)

    b. Variation 2: Start in the vertical seam and traverse left into the problem. (V6)

4. *Hands of the Potter: Start on a vertical seam and sloper. Move straight up, past a pocket and sloper to a sidepull. Move off the sidepull past another pocket and gaston to a sloping jug to finish. Avoid the letterbox jug out right. (V3)

    a. Variation: Start as described above, but move right to a letterbox jug. Continue

A young Carl Samples cruises Woody's Arête in the attire of the day. PHOTO COURTESY OF CARL SAMPLES

7. **Ball's Out: Establish on the large "Cannonball" pocket and ascend the thin face to the roof. Downclimb the problem or make a frightful traverse left to *Woody's Arête* and downclimb there. A great problem, but the retreat is death! (V5) (BL SHB)

   a. *Phenomenace: Start on the large pocket, but traverse right through thin moves, finishing on the right arête. (V5)

   b. Spiderwoman Problem: Locate the large pocket in the center of the face. Step off the rock and stand up in the pocket, using no hands. Quite fun! (VB)

Note: The next 40 feet of slab has been bouldered or climbed to the roof. The climbing on these faces is quite good, however, there is no easy way to descend and the landings are quite bad. Boulder these at your own risk.

Area 2: Mr. Clean Corridor

Be sure to scope and clean the topouts for the problems on this face before trying them.

8. **Black Bart: On the back side of the Rotting Log is this short little problem. Start on a low jug and follow edges up the overhanging face, avoiding the left arête. (V3) (SS TO)

   a. Variation: Does not avoid the holds on the arête. (V1) (SS TO)

9. ***Scar: Thin-feet and body-tension oriented! Start standing on the talus on your choice of holds. Move up and left to a sloping horizontal. Continue left across the improving horizontal, finishing left. (V3) (TO BL)

   a. **Coopers Rockette: Adds the direct start. Start on the ground left of the talus and make a difficult move through a sloping edge to join the normal variation at the horizontal. (V6) (TO BL)

10. *Dark Serpent: Make an awkward establish on a triangular hold. Continue past a pocket to the top. (V6) (TO)

11. *Jump: Jump-start to a horizontal in the center of the tall face (black streak). Continue through horizontals to the top. (V2) (TO HB BL)

   a. *Variation: Start on the large talus and traverse into the normal problem. (V2) (TO HB BL)

Area 3

Across the gap from *Woody's Arête,* on the right side of the Mr. Clean Face, are three problems. These problems are high, however, the difficulty of the bouldering is low. These problems are easily protected by one crash pad.

12. Start on two high pockets and make a hard move past an edge to a pocket. Either finish on the jug or continue through benign holds to the top. (V4) (HB)

   a. Variation: Adds the low start. (V5) (HB)

13. **Start about 4 feet left of the tree on pockets and/or a sloper. Make a long move to a decent edge and continue with a thin move. Finish through sloping, but mellow jugs to the top. (V3) (HB)

14. *Start just right of the previous problem on a pocket and shared pinch. Move up past a sidepull to a sloper. Continue through slopers to the top. (V2) (HB)

Boulder 4: The Wheel

15. The Wheel: If you're into awkward roofs, look no further. Start on the jug and make a long move out past a sloper to a horizontal. Power off the horizontal to the top. The flat rock is off. (V5) (TO BL)

Jimi Cliff

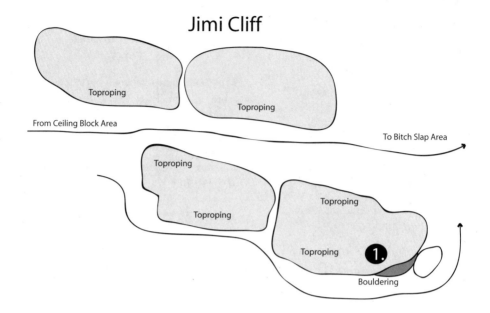

Jimi Cliff Area (aka Sunset Walls)

To reach the Jimi Cliff Area, continue down the main trail, past the Ceiling Block Area, for about 200 yards. The Jimi Cliff Area is mainly a toproping area; however, there are a handful of good boulder problems on the second Big Block. Some of these problems add low starts and variations to already-established toprope routes.

Boulder 1: Big Block 2

1. ★★Start on the first obvious jug in the white area and move up and left to a sloping rail. Make a powerful move directly past a thin edge and sloping horizontal to a jug. Finish on the jug just over the small roof. (V4) (SS)

2. ★★Start on a sloper and incut flake. Move up past a flake to a jug. Continue slightly left, finishing on the small ledge about a foot over the roof. (V3) (SS)

3. ★A little forced, but very body-tension oriented. Suck into a difficult establish matched on a knob and edge. Make a strenuous move (or throw) up and right to a jug, finishing on the horizontal below the roof. Avoid the undercling mentioned in the variation. (V5)

   a. *★Variation:* Reminiscent of the McConnell's Mill Classic: Wonder World. Start on the same sidepull but utilize an undercling out right. Throw for the jug and finish as normal. (V3)

4. ★★**Great White Rasta:** Start on two slopers and move up past an edge to a sidepull. Continue left, finishing just right of the previous problem. Note: You can also move right off the sidepull and finish on the next problem (same grade). (V0+)

5. ★★**White Wall Overhang:** Start on a low sloper (matched) and move up past a knob to another sloper. Continue past a horizontal, finishing below the roof. (V3)

6. ★★Start on an incut jug and continue directly up over the bulge past jugs to the

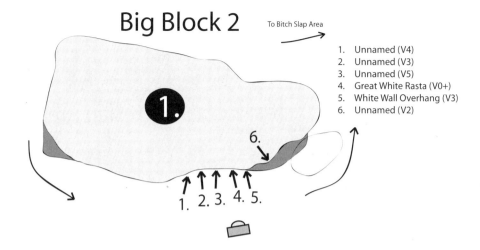

Big Block 2

To Bitch Slap Area →

1. Unnamed (V4)
2. Unnamed (V3)
3. Unnamed (V5)
4. Great White Rasta (V0+)
5. White Wall Overhang (V3)
6. Unnamed (V2)

ledge. You have to top out at least once to get the tick. (V2) (TO)

a. **Variation: Start on the same jug, but follow sidepulls and underclings out

Vicky Arthur on Big Block 2. PHOTO BY BOB ARTHUR

right. Move back left and then continue up and right through the subtle nose of handlebars to the ledge. You have to top out at least once to get the tick. (V3) (TO)

Bitch Slap Area

The Bitch Slap Area has several super-classic boulder problems. The compression problem *Bitch Slap Arête* (V5+) and its slabby companion *Donkey Punch* (V3) should not be missed.

To reach the Bitch Slap Area, continue down the trail from the Jimi Cliff Area for about 200 yards. Follow the trail past several small boulders, trending left over a big log. Continue past a large overhanging block on your left (The Diamond). Make a left around this block to reach problem 1.

Boulder 1: The Diamond

1. **Where does it end? Good question. Start on an incut jug and move up to another jug. Ascend the arête, moving past a pocket and an edge to a letterbox. End here (V5), or continue if you dare. Consider hidden edges to mellow out the sequence. (V5) (SS BL)

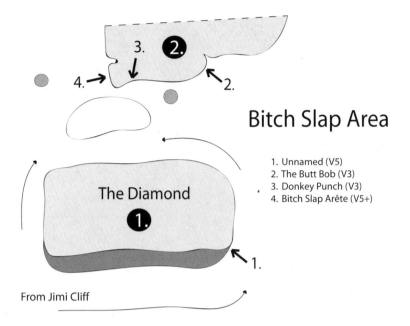

Bitch Slap Area

1. Unnamed (V5)
2. The Butt Bob (V3)
3. Donkey Punch (V3)
4. Bitch Slap Arête (V5+)

The Diamond

From Jimi Cliff

Boulder 2:
Bitch Slap Boulder

2. *The Butt Bob: Where is the oddest place you've ever had sex? Start just left of the crack and make a hard move to the jug. Everything right of the crack is off. (V3) (SS TO)

    a. *Variation: Does not avoid feet right of the crack. (V1) (SS TO)

3. ***Donkey Punch: A super-smeary classic! Start a few feet left of the large tree on a sidepull and undercling. Make a super-flexible move to a good edge. Move out left, past a good rail to the top. (V3) (TO BL HB)

4. ****Bitch Slap Arête: The classic "compression strength" line in the forest. Start on slopers and claw your way up the overhanging prow. Make several compression and scum moves past a good pocket to the top. Everything to the left of the crack is off. (V5+) (TO)

    a. ****Variation: Eliminates the sit-start. (V5) (SS TO)

Sponge Bob Rentka pounding up *Bitch Slap Arête.* PHOTO BY CARL SAMPLES

UPPER ROCK CITY

Directions: From the main gate, drive 2.6 miles until you reach the concession stand parking lot (dead end). Park here and follow the trail on the left side of the concession stand, passing the pay phone and water fountain. Continue down this trail for about 30 yards, trending left toward the cliff. You will see a set of stone-carved stairs on your left that is posted RATTLESNAKE TRAIL. Continue down through these stairs, past several boulders to a trail intersection. Either turn left and head directly down the hill toward the large block "Forgotten Block" or continue right to access the other areas.

The Upper Rock City area features a host of high-quality boulder problems, mostly in the V3–V5 range. The problems in this area are Coopers Rock typical highballs, however, a disproportionate amount are sit-starts. Some classic problems are *Colorful Corner* (V4), *Tomb Raider* (V3), *Big Block Nose*

(V4), and *Roundhouse* (V5). One notable problem, *Fire Warning* (V8), was established by an unknown Englishman circa 1972.

The Holy Face

A tribute to the coveted and secret "SO-Ill" bouldering area, this boulder features four highball, quality problems.

To reach this area, continue down the stone steps to a fork in the trail. Veer right and look for the clean face hidden behind a small boulder.

Boulder 1: The Holy Face

This face features four high-quality but sketchy problems. **Be sure that you are solid at the grade before trying these problems.** Also, the trees make the landings for several of these problems quite impossible. Be sure to walk around and scope the topouts of these problems before trying them.

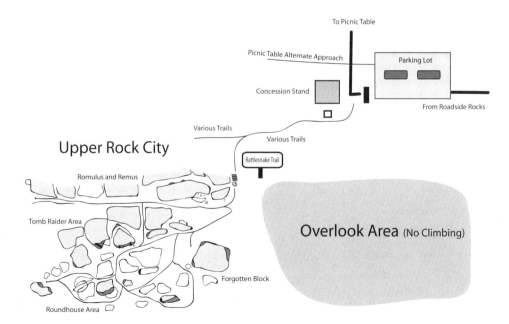

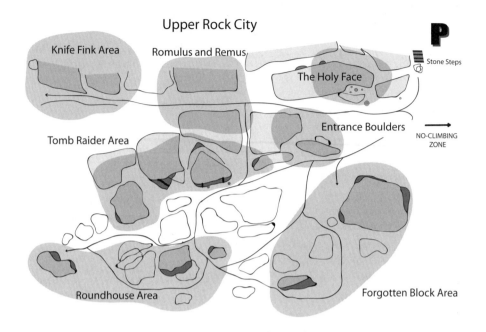

Upper Rock City

Knife Fink Area

Romulus and Remus

The Holy Face

P

Stone Steps

Entrance Boulders

→

NO-CLIMBING ZONE

Tomb Raider Area

Roundhouse Area

Forgotten Block Area

1. **Say Your Prayers: Start 2 feet right of the tree on two high, deep jugs. Continue up the face past a sidepull, through horizontals to the top. (V0+) (TO SHB BL)

2. **The Beautiful Letdown: Painfully unclear! Start just left of the tree on a left-facing sidepull. Make a thin move to a horizontal and continue through insecure horizontals up and slightly left to the top. Be sure

to clean the back rail for the topout. (V3) (TO SHB BL)

3. **Suddenly: Start in front of the large tree on a left-facing sidepull. Make a long move past a mono to a horizontal. Continue past a rad sidepull and trend left through horizontals to a huge pocket. Finish with a straightforward topout. (V3) (SS TO SHB BL)

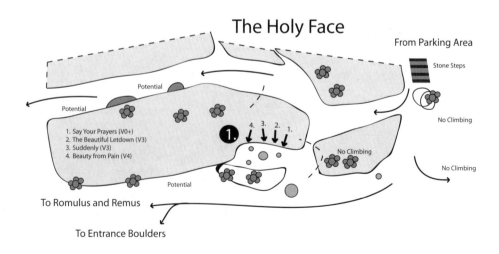

The Holy Face

From Parking Area

Stone Steps

Potential

Potential

No Climbing

1. Say Your Prayers (V0+)
2. The Beautiful Letdown (V3)
3. Suddenly (V3)
4. Beauty from Pain (V4)

1.

4. 3. 2. 1.

No Climbing

No Climbing

Potential

To Romulus and Remus ←

To Entrance Boulders

4. ***Beauty from Pain: A soft but quality V4. Start on a right sidepull and step up to edges. Make a long move off edges to a horizontal and then make another long move to a jug. Continue up and then slightly left on sloping horizontals and a pocket. Finish just left of the tree. (V4) (TO SHB BL)

Entrance Boulders (aka Warm-up Boulders)

The Entrance Boulders feature several good moderate problems as well as several decent hard problems. To reach the entrance boulders, travel down the main trail for about 20 yards. Cut left through the talus and a fir tree to reach Boulder 2.

Boulder 1

The best retreat for the next five problems is the downhill side of the boulder.

1. No Surprise: Start on the arête on a pocket and undercling. Continue up the slab on mossy slopers, trending right for the topout. (V1) (HB BL TO)

2. *Surprise: An old toprope route graded accordingly (much harder than V0!). Start 3 feet left of the arête on sidepulls. Make a thin move up past a horizontal to a jug sidepull. Continue directly up the face to a shared finish with the previous problem. (V0) (HB BL TO)

3. *BBW: With a little traffic, this would be a classic. Start on the obvious right-facing flake. Continue up the gently overhanging face past edges and horizontals to the top. (V0+) (HB TO)

4. **U.R.S.T.: Unresolved sexual tension. When it builds up, you just need to blow some of it off! A great sloper problem. Start on a horizontal and sidepull. Ascend the overhanging arête past an edge and textbook slopers to the top. (V2) (SS TO)

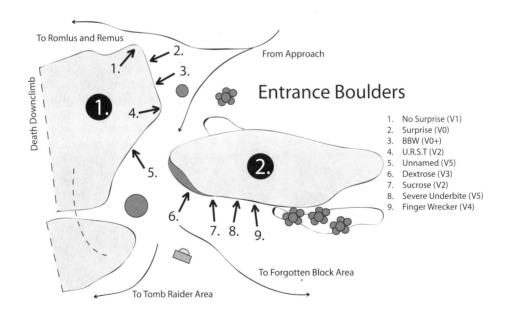

Entrance Boulders

1. No Surprise (V1)
2. Surprise (V0)
3. BBW (V0+)
4. U.R.S.T (V2)
5. Unnamed (V5)
6. Dextrose (V3)
7. Sucrose (V2)
8. Severe Underbite (V5)
9. Finger Wrecker (V4)

5. With some traffic, this would be a great problem. Start on a left-facing edge. Move up past a sloping edge and make a long move for the sloping top. (V5) (SS TO)

Boulder 2:
Have It Your Way Boulder

To view the topography of problems 6 through 9, see the topo below.

6. **Dextrose: Start matched on the left-most jug under the small roof. Move out right pasts edges and make a powerful set of moves up past a pristine pinch and sidepull to another pocket. Make a long move for the top, finishing just right of the small tree. (V3) (SS TO)

    a. **Font-tastic: We guess the French manage to get some things right every now and then. Start on the same jug, but instead, slap up and left over the blunt overhanging prow, past a pocket to the top. (V4) (SS TO)

7. *Sucrose: Start on an undercling or your choice of pockets and move up and slightly right, past a vertical pocket. Power up and left to a jug. *Note:* This problem can share some holds with the previous problem. (V2) (TO)

    a. **Variation Start—Nutra-Sweet: Traverse in from the start of the previous problem and finish as normal. (V3) (SS TO)

8. **Severe Underbite: Start on a letterbox and edge. Move up past sloping sidepulls through a questionable left-facing flake to the top. (V5) (SS TO)

    a. **Happy-Happy Sugar Slab: Eliminates the sit-start. (V2) (TO)

    b. **Sugar Daddy: Stand-start the same, but move up and left past small pockets to a large vertical pocket. Continue up and left, joining Sucrose for the finish. (V3) (SS TO)

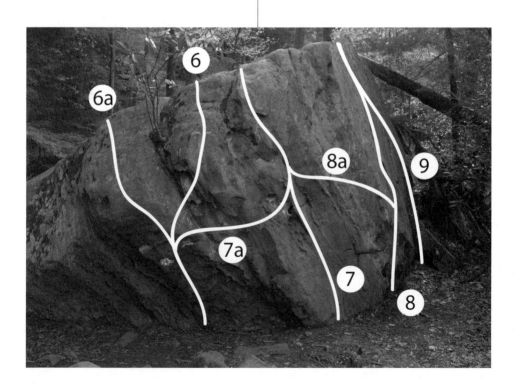

9. * Finger Wrecker (aka Career Ender):

Named after the injury sustained one try before the FA via the sit-start. Start on an incut flake and upper pocket. Make a difficult move past a thin edge, slopers, and bad feet to a stance and an edge. Follow a shared finish to the top. (V4) (SS TO)

Romulus and Remus Area

The Romulus and Remus Area has a host of both moderate and difficult problems. The *Colorful Corner* (V4) is a must-do arête. The *Ray Charles Traverse* (V3+) is also quite good. To reach the Romulus and Remus Area, continue along the main trail from the initial fork for about 70 yards until you see the striking orange arête *(Colorful Corner)*.

Boulder 1:
Romulus and Remus Face

The standard downclimb for these problems is the broken crack system about 10 feet left

Tim Keenan on *Finger Wrecker.*

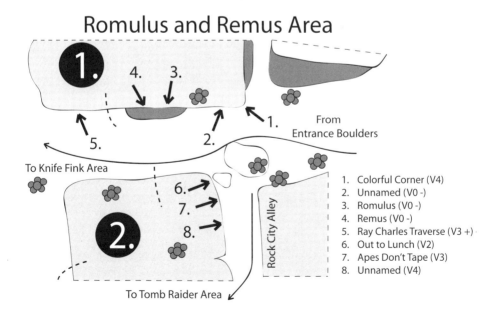

Romulus and Remus Area

1. Colorful Corner (V4)
2. Unnamed (V0 -)
3. Romulus (V0 -)
4. Remus (V0 -)
5. Ray Charles Traverse (V3 +)
6. Out to Lunch (V2)
7. Apes Don't Tape (V3)
8. Unnamed (V4)

The Sith on *Colorful Corner.* PHOTO BY CARL SAMPLES

of Remus. The Romulus and Remus face is lavished with good holds, making for a host of moderate problems and eliminates.

1. ★★★★Colorful Corner (aka Stevie Wonder Arête): What a great problem! Start on a large edge and continue up past thin edges and sidepulls to a jug. Either traverse off left and downclimb or follow pleasant but thrilling moves on big holds to the top. (V4) (TO HB)

    a. ★★Variation: Contrived, but a good variation. Start on the triangular pocket and continue past thin edges to an iron rail. Finish on the upper ledge and either top out or downclimb. (V3) (TO HB)

2. ★★Commonly toproped, a good highball for the New Wave crash-pad-packing mongrels. Start about 7 feet left of the arête and

just right of a protruding boulder on edges. Make a long move past edges to a horizontal. Make another long move to a horizontal and downclimb. (V0–) (HB)

3. ★★Romulus: The complementary toproped route that can be bouldered. Start in front of the talus and continue past edges and horizontals to a flake. Power off the flake to a horizontal under the roof. Downclimb. (V0–) (HB)

    a. Variation: Start just right of the previous problem, just left of a stump, and follow edges to a long move for the horizontal. Downclimb. (V0–) (HB)

4. ★★Remus: Start left of center under the large roof on a horizontal. Make a long move to an edge and continue past horizontals and a sidepull to a pocket. Finish on a jug under the roof and make a delicate traverse left on a polished horizontal to the downclimb. (V0–) (HB)

5. ★★Ray Charles Traverse (aka Helen Keller Traverse): Start just right of the log on large holds. Move right across the face following good horizontals and thin feet. Continue to a blind, powerful move around the arête. Make several more moves on incut holds and finish. *Note:* This problem can be bouldered from right to left at the same grade. (V3+)

Boulder 2

One can either walk-off or retreat down the often wet and mossy but easy crack system (Crisco Crack), which faces the Romulus and Remus Boulder. Be sure to pad or have a spotter for this downclimb: It is about 25 to 30 feet and not completely straightforward.

6. ★★Out to Lunch: Start on two small edges and move up past a sidepull to a good edge. Make a long move off edges to a jug and follow large, often dirty, jugs to the top. A good edgy problem reminiscent of *Strike a Scowl* at the New River Gorge. Using the tree for the topout is the acceptable style. (V2) (HB BL TO)

7. **Apes Don't Tape: An awkward problem that recently had a hold break. Start on a good ring-lock and move up through a devious sequence past edges and gastons to a jug. Either jump off from the jug or traverse right and finish on *Out to Lunch*. (V3) (BL)

8. Ascend the right-facing flake crack to a jug and finish. (V4)

Knife Fink Area

A large area with a handful of quality problems. Continue on the trail past Romulus and Remus for about 20 yards. You will see an overhanging face on your right. This is the Knife Fink Boulder. If you continue past this block, there is a whole maze of boulders that eventually leads to the Picnic Table Boulder (another section of this book).

Boulder 1: Knife Fink Boulder

The best retreat for these problems is to hop across to the Romulus and Remus Boulder and downclimb there.

1. **Man Eating Bitch: A tall, aesthetic line characterized by good holds separated by long reaches. Start on a high horizontal and ascend the proud face past a pocket to a horizontal jug. Continue past edges to a frightful but straightforward move to the top. (V2) (SHB TO)

The problems on the Knife Fink face tend to share feet with other problems. Also, the topouts on these problems can be difficult; don't cheat and use the tree!

2.****Knife Fink: Ethereal moves, but the landing is total death! If V1 is your limit, be sure to have a spotter to make this problem safe. Start on an edge and move up the arête to the ledge. (V1) (SS TO BL)

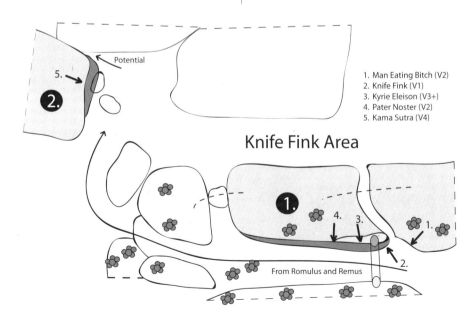

1. Man Eating Bitch (V2)
2. Knife Fink (V1)
3. Kyrie Eleison (V3+)
4. Pater Noster (V2)
5. Kama Sutra (V4)

Knife Fink Area

From Romulus and Remus

Bob Rentka on *Knife Fink.*

3. **Kyrie Eleison: Start on sloper and power up to a horizontal. Continue up and right past a horizontal and pockets, finishing with a press mantel just left of the leaning tree. (V3+) (SS TO BL)

To the left of *Kyrie Eleison* is a good problem (*Christe Eleison,* V5), which is, unfortunately, eternally wet.

4. **Pater Noster: Start on a left-facing flake and continue up past edges, making a long move to a sloper. Continue past a horizontal, finishing with a sketchy topout. (V2) (SS TO BL)

Boulder 2

To reach the next problem, continue down the trail for about 100 feet until you reach an opening. Trend right toward the "cave" to locate this obvious line.

5. ***Kama Sutra: A great power problem. Start on two edges just left of the angled talus. Traverse right on edges to two incut edges. Make a long move for a sloper, match, and make another long move to a horizontal to finish. Be sure to have a spotter: The landing for the throws can result in ankle injuries. (V4) (SS RBL)

Tomb Raider Area

One of the most concentrated areas in Upper Rock City is the Tomb Raider Area. This area features a host of mostly difficult problems. *Tomb Raider* (V3), the newly estab-

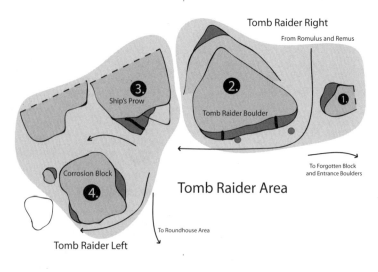

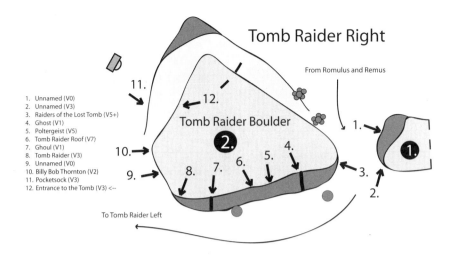

Tomb Raider Right

1. Unnamed (V0)
2. Unnamed (V3)
3. Raiders of the Lost Tomb (V5+)
4. Ghost (V1)
5. Poltergeist (V5)
6. Tomb Raider Roof (V7)
7. Ghoul (V1)
8. Tomb Raider (V3)
9. Unnamed (V0)
10. Billy Bob Thornton (V2)
11. Pocketsock (V3)
12. Entrance to the Tomb (V3) <--

From Romulus and Remus

Tomb Raider Boulder

To Tomb Raider Left

lished *Raiders of the Lost Tomb* (V5+), and *Tomb Raider Roof* (V7) are classics. If you like pain, consider the overhanging cracks *(Ghost and Ghoul)* on the Tomb Raider Boulder.

Since this area is so large, it has been broken into two map sections: Tomb Raider Left and Tomb Raider Right.

Boulder 1:
Warm-up Boulder

1. *Start on a jug and follow the short line of pockets top. (V0) (SS TO)

2. Start on a sloping jug on the arête and follow the short arête to the crux topout. (V3) (SS TO)

Boulder 2:
Tomb Raider Boulder

3. ***Raiders of the Lost Tomb: Yet another problem to fall into the V5 sand trap, but what a great problem! Start on a good pocket and thin sloper. Move up and left through pristine slopers and sidepulls to a heartbreaker topout. (V5+) (SS TO)

4. Ghost: Not often traveled, this crack is generally grimy. Tape up and ascend the gnarly off-width. Get nasty with it! (V1) (SS TO)

5. *Poltergeist: Ascend the overhanging face past jugs to the crux topout. Either jump or trudge up the lichen to the top. (V5) (TO)

Dan Brayack on *Raiders of the Lost Tomb.*
PHOTO BY ADAM WISTHOFF

6. ***Tomb Raider Roof: Really good if it's ever dry, but then, it's never dry, so do it wet! Start on pockets and slopers and move up through edges, slopers, and jugs to a grimacing topout. (V7) (SS TO)

a. ***Variation: Eliminates the sit-start. (V5) (TO)

7. Ghoul: Not often traveled, this crack generally needs some love. Tape up and ascend the masochistic overhanging fist crack to the top. (V1) (SS TO)

8. ****Tomb Raider: Start on an undercling and sidepull pocket. Move up past a sidepull, out right to the "Lara Croft" sloper. Make a long move to an undercling jug and finish.

Most boulderers jump from the jug, but you have to top out once to get the tick. (V3) (SS TO)

a. *Variation Start: The anti-height-dependant problem. Start matched on the undercling and continue as described above. (V5) (SS TO)

9. Ascend the center of the face past sloping horizontals as high as you dare. If you plan to top out, trend right at the top. A good one to get the blood flowing and the brain clear. (V0) (HB TO)

10. **Billy Bob Thornton (aka Brad Pitt): Start on a jug and undercling. Make aesthetic moves up and slightly right past sidepulls and

a hand-foot match, following the nose to a jug and finish matched (V1). Or make several hairball moves to a mellow scramble and walk-off. For best quality, finish sans topout. (V2) (SS TO HB)

The following problems all share the same start, but each variation finishes differently.

To view the topography of problem 11 and its variations, see the topo on p. 72.

11. **Pocketsock: Start on pockets and continue up and slightly left through edges and thin pockets, past an incut pocket to the top. (V3) (SS TO)

   a. *Variation 1: Start as normal, but continue up and right past a sloping edge and pocket, following left-facing edges and pockets to the top. (V3) (SS TO)

   b. *Variation 2: Start as normal, but at midheight move 10 feet left to another set of pockets and continue to the top. (V4) (SS TO)

   c. Variation 3: From variation 2, continue traversing left to a good sidepull and sloping pocket. Top out through the rail. (V6) (SS HB TO BL)

12. *Entrance to the Tomb: Start on a pocket and sloper and follow the crack left to the blunt corner. Finish over the blunt corner. A great 2-foot-high traverse, if you're into that sort of thing. (V3) (SS TO)

Boulder 3: Ship's Prow

To view the topography of problems 13 through 17a, see the topo on p. 74.

13. **A Touch of Tango: A good, aesthetic problem with big moves between good holds. Start on an edge and sidepull and move up past another sidepull to a jug. Continue past a thin horizontal and finish on the ledge just right of the roof. (V2) (SS)

Tomb Raider Left

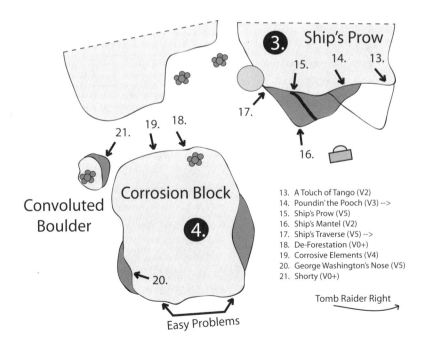

13. A Touch of Tango (V2)
14. Poundin' the Pooch (V3) -->
15. Ship's Prow (V5)
16. Ship's Mantel (V2)
17. Ship's Traverse (V5) -->
18. De-Forestation (V0+)
19. Corrosive Elements (V4)
20. George Washington's Nose (V5)
21. Shorty (V0+)

Tomb Raider Right

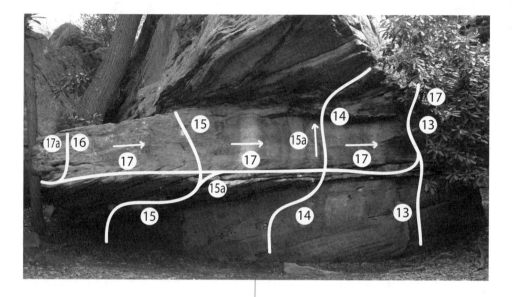

14. **Poundin' the Pooch: Start on an undercling or monos under the right side of the low roof. Move up, traversing right, through horizontals to a long move for a sloper. Move up to a horizontal under the roof and continue up and right, finishing on the ledge. (V3) (SS TO)

15. ****Ship's Prow: A great roof problem! Start on a loose jug and follow the line of edges using siege foot tactics. Continue past an undercling to a jug at the first lip. Finish with a burly huck for the top. (V5) (SS TO)

    a. **Variation: Instead of moving to the top at the first lip, follow the horizontals right to join and finish on *Poundin' the Pooch.* (V5+) (SS TO)

16. *Ship's Mantel: Start on the arête and move up and right past a horizontal and pockets, finishing just right of the arête. (V2) (TO)

17. *Ship's Traverse: Start just right of the tree on an edge and traverse right across the lip to finish on *A Touch of Tango.* (V5) (SS)

    a. **Variation Finish: A pumpy traverse coupled with an aesthetic finish. Start as

described above, but finish on the *Ship's Mantel* (problem 16). (V3) (SS TO)

Boulder 4: Corrosion Block

18. ***De-Forestation: A great moderate problem! Ascend the left-facing flake and crack past a jug to the top. Top out just left of the tree. (V0+) (TO)

19. **Corrosive Element: Start on the obvious incut jug. Move up and right, and then slightly back left through slopers, pockets, and a sidepull to a harrowing topout move. Be sure to scout the topout "edge." (V4) (SS HB TO)

20. ***George Washington's Nose (aka C.O.T.D.): A great body-tension-oriented power problem. Start on a jug under the roof. Make a long move over the roof to an edge. Traverse left, past a seam and small roof, and finish on the incut jug just over the roof. Be sure to check the moisture situation of the key foot for the traverse before investing energy on this problem. (V5) (SS)

Vicky Arthur on *Ship's Prow.* PHOTO BY BOB ARTHUR

Convoluted Boulder

This small roof has a host of great holds spurring endless variations and eliminates.

21. **Shorty: Short, but great moves! Start on the right side of the small boulder on a sidepull and pockets. Continue up and left on pockets to the nose. The topout is optional for this problem and its variations. (V0+) (SS)

   a. **Sorry Shorty: A good problem for only two moves! Start on a left slanting horizontal in the center of the boulder and power up to a good pinch. Power off the pinch to the top. (V1) (SS)

   b. **Not So Shorty: Almost independent, this problem shares the finish with the previous problems. Lay-down start as low as you can (sans crash pad) in the leaves on the left side of the boulder. Move up and left to a large pocket. Make powerful moves past edges and a pocket to the top. (V2) (SS)

Forgotten Block Area (aka Lost Block)

The Forgotten Block, or the "Lost Block" as featured in *Gritstone Climbs,* by Bill Webster (1978), features a score of "newly" developed problems. The problems on this boulder tend to be highballs, so be sure to pad accordingly. Some of the classics on this block are *Myxomatosis* (V6), *Pentagon* (V7), *Jacob's Ladder* (V4), and *Big Block Nose* (V4).

   To reach the Forgotten Block Area, follow the Rattlesnake Trail for about 30 yards from the initial split.

Boulder 1: Forgotten Block (aka Lost Block)

The most reasonable retreat from this boulder is the *Big Block Nose* (be sure to pad for the jump). Another retreat is the molar arête, which is easily downclimbed to a jumpable height (also be sure to pad).

To view the topography of problems 1 through 3, see the topo on p. 77.

1. Pearly Gates: Start on the jug in front of the daunting tree. Move up past a good sidepull through thinning slopers and sidepulls to the top. Don't bother spotting your buddy on this one: If he/she blows it, you'll be needed to help with the carry-out. (V4) (SHB RBL TO)

2. **Jacob's Ladder: High and scary, but really good! Start on a jug about 5 feet left of the tree. Make a hard move up past a crack to a good horizontal. Ascend harrowing sidepulls and slopers to the top. (V4) (SS TO SHB)

    a. ***Myxomatosis: Start as normal, but traverse left at the large seam (about 12 feet up) for 15 feet (crux) until you reach two large pockets. Get a good shake and ascend the thin face past pockets and sloping edges to the top. (V6) (SS SHB TO)

3. ***Big Block Nose: A good problem to show off your bubble-butt. Start on a good flake and make a long move up right to a pocket. Move back left on pockets and paw your way up the arête to a jug. (V4) (SS)

4. **Pentagon: Start on a good pocket and edge about 15 feet left of the arête. Power up to a sloper. Make several desperate moves through grim slopers, and continue on easy terrain to the top. See if you can spot the origin of the name. (V7) (SS TO)

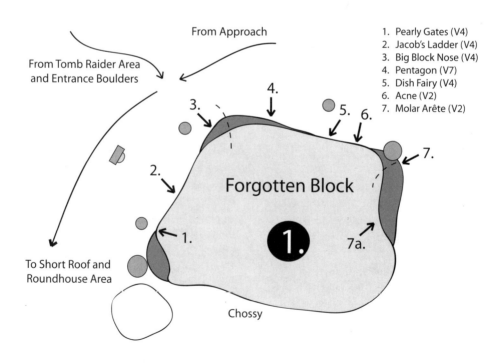

From Approach

From Tomb Raider Area and Entrance Boulders

1. Pearly Gates (V4)
2. Jacob's Ladder (V4)
3. Big Block Nose (V4)
4. Pentagon (V7)
5. Dish Fairy (V4)
6. Acne (V2)
7. Molar Arête (V2)

Forgotten Block

To Short Roof and Roundhouse Area

Chossy

Tim Keenan groping at the crux of *Pentagon*.

5. *Dish Fairy:* Start underneath a short crack just left of a small fir tree. Step up to an undercling and sloper and make a long move to the ledge. Continue through slabby ledges to the top. (V4) (HB TO)

6. Acne: Start on an undercling and pinch jug. Continue up and left past a good pocket, trending left through the line of least resistance to the top. (V2) (HB TO)

7. *Molar Arête:* Start on the left side of the arête on a horizontal. Move up past a layaway to a sloping horizontal on the arête. Continue up the arête on jugs, trending right toward the top. (V2) (TO HB)

    a. **Wisdom Teeth:* Start about 20 feet left of the Molar Arête. Traverse under the roof on slopers and edges, finishing up the arête. (V6) (SS TO HB)

Boulder 2: Short Roof

To reach the next boulder, continue down the trail past the Forgotten Block. Proceed

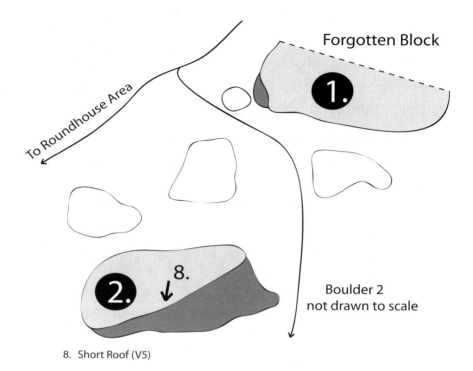

8. Short Roof (V5)

off the trail, past a chossy rock, over several small boulders. Continue down and right to reach the Short Roof.

8. **Short Roof: Start on an incut edge and small edge. Power out the roof to the lip. Traverse right across the lip past pockets, an upper edge, and a good pocket, finishing up the blunt right corner. (V5) (SS TO)

    a. Variation: Start as described above, but continue out left past small pockets to the top. (V3) (SS TO)

Roundhouse Area

The Roundhouse Area features a handful of high-quality difficult problems. Roundhouse (V5) is one of the best power problems in the forest. To reach the Roundhouse Area, trend down the hill from the Tomb Raider Boulder, passing a large flat boulder (Blue

Blazes–Rattlesnake Trail). Roundhouse is the obvious line out the center of the overhanging face. *Note:* The Roundhouse Boulder was originally called the "Lost Block" in the *Gritstone Climbs,* by Bill Webster (1978). Also, *Pure Power* is listed as a 5.7 climb!

**1. **Start matched backwards on the first edge. Power out the roof to a jug at the lip. Continue out right, past pockets and an edge, finishing just left of the tree. The back block is off. (V3) (SS TO)

Boulder 1: Roundhouse Boulder (aka the Lost Block)

2. **Pure Power: Ascend the physical flake to a honkin' "hero-hang" jug. *Note:* This problem uses feet on Roundhouse. Also, ending on the jug is advisable since the topout "jugs" are

Roundhouse Boulder

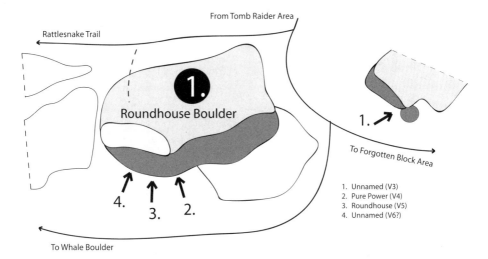

Rattlesnake Trail

From Tomb Raider Area

1.
Roundhouse Boulder

1.

To Forgotten Block Area

4. 3. 2.

To Whale Boulder

1. Unnamed (V3)
2. Pure Power (V4)
3. Roundhouse (V5)
4. Unnamed (V6?)

sandy and friable and the topout does not add anything to the problem. (V4) (SS)

3. ****Roundhouse: Soft for V5, but then, you cannot win them all. Start on a jug and move out left, past a sidepull to a pinch. Make a core-intensive move past a right-facing flake (feet usually kick) to a thin but straightforward topout. (V5) (SS TO)

**4. **Start on a right-facing flake. Move up and left, past a pocket to a sloping lip. Make a really hard topout move and finish. (V6?) (SS TO)

Boulder 2: Whale Boulder

To reach the Whale Boulder, continue past the Roundhouse Boulder down the Rattlesnake Trail for about 50 yards. *Note:* Some of these grades might be soft.

5. Blow Hole: Start on a good edge and continue through several slopers to a mellow finish. (V4) (SS TO)

6. *Whale's Belly: Since a hold broke, this problem has become more difficult. Start on

Whale Boulder

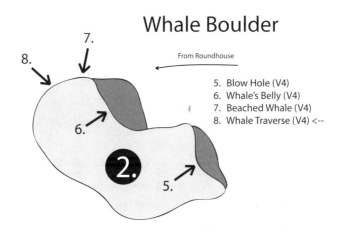

7.

8.

From Roundhouse

5. Blow Hole (V4)
6. Whale's Belly (V4)
7. Beached Whale (V4)
8. Whale Traverse (V4) <--

2.

6.

5.

an incut flake and ascend the steep face past an edge and pinch to a thin topout. The left wall is obviously off. (V4) (SS TO)

7. *Beached Whale: Start on right-facing edges. Make a hard move for the top and partake in the "Beached Whale" topout. (V4) (SS TO)

8. Whale Traverse: Quite strenuous. Start on the furthest sloper and traverse left to finish on *Whale's Belly* (problem 6). (V4) (SS TO)

PICNIC TABLE (MUSHROOM BOULDER)

Directions: From the main gate, drive 2.4 miles until you see a gate on your right. If you reach a large parking lot with a kiosk on the left, you've gone too far. Make a right, go through the gate, and proceed down the hill. Park at the bottom of the loop. Travel a short distance down the Ridge Trail; the Picnic Boulder is the large chalk-covered roof up the hill on the left.

Alternate approach: If the gate is closed, you can either hike down the road, or for a more scenic and less arduous approach, continue to and park at the concession stand (dead-end of main road). Travel just right of the concession stand and continue down the well-established

Picnic Table Boulder

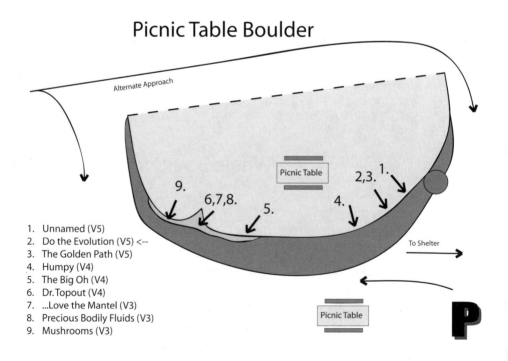

1. Unnamed (V5)
2. Do the Evolution (V5) <--
3. The Golden Path (V5)
4. Humpy (V4)
5. The Big Oh (V4)
6. Dr. Topout (V4)
7. ...Love the Mantel (V3)
8. Precious Bodily Fluids (V3)
9. Mushrooms (V3)

Vicky Arthur working through *The Golden Path*. PHOTO BY BOB ARTHUR

trail. Cross a large trail and continue for about 300 yards until you see a large shelter. Head toward this shelter—the Picnic Table Boulder is on the way to the shelter.

The Picnic Table Boulder offers a host of powerful roof problems coupled with sloping topouts. With its close proximity to the parking area, this boulder is a good stop for a short, powerful session. During tourist season it is advisable to avoid this boulder due to sight and noise impact to other forest user groups. The problems on this boulder are generally the last in the forest to dry. However, they are often done in the "dank" state.

The retreat for all problems here is a simple walkoff.

1. ★★Start on a sloper under the first obvious chalk line out the roof. Make several delightful moves through good holds to a sloper.

Make a deceptively hard grunt past a pocket and slopers to the top. (V5) (SS TO)

   a. ★★Variation Finish: From the sloper at the lip, continue left to another sloper and finish. (V5) (SS TO)

2. ★★★Do the Evolution: A multicruxing pumpfest! Start on the same sloper as the previous problem but traverse low left, entertaining big moves past increasingly positive holds. Be sure to catch a good rest and continue to a heartbreaker finish up Mushrooms. Don't bother padding "Mt. Vesuvius"—save the pad for the finish. (V5) (SS TO)

3. ★★★The Golden Path: A foot-beta problem. Start just left of the previous problem on slopers. Utilizing a frightful foot-jam, make a big move out left to a "flexing" jug. Make another big move to an often wet jug and continue (using siege tactics) past an edge to a strenuous mantel. (V5) (SS TO)

Scotty Dahl lining up for *The Golden Path.*

4. ***Humpy: Once you do the topout, you'll understand the name. Start on a sloper under the widest point of the roof. Make powerful moves through small edges, past a pinch to a jug. Make a rather degrading topout move and rejoice. (V4) (SS TO)

To view the topography of problems 2 and 5 through 9, see the topo on p. 83.

5. **The Big Oh: Start about 20 feet left of Humpy at the start of the large sloping ledge. Move out left past an incut horn and setup with a key heel hook. Make a strenuous move past a right-facing sidepull, through an undercling to the top. Trend slightly right for the topout. (V4) (SS TO)

The next three problems share the start. The first moves several feet right, the second stays just right of the crack, and the third stays left of the crack.

6. **Dr. Topout: Start below the crack on two large edges and continue right past ledges and pinch to an undercling. Continue past a pocket to the top. Move right to a decent horn and topout. (V4) (SS TO)

7. ***or How I Learned How to Stop Worrying and Love the Mantel: A really aesthetic, flowing problem . . . up until the topout. Start below the crack on two large edges and continue straight up and then slightly left, past a ledge through edges, an undercling, and a sloper. Move left into the crack and mantel. Avoid using the left side of the crack for both feet and body friction. (V3) (SS TO)

    a. ***Variation Finish: A more direct and clean finish. From the sloper, continue directly over the top. (V5) (SS TO)

8. **Precious Bodily Fluids: Start matched; move up and left on horizontals. Set up with

a key heel hook and slap up the blunt prow moving through slopey edges to a sloper, and finish left. (V3) (SS TO)

9. ****Mushrooms: One of the best problems in the forest at the grade! Start on a jug and pinch below obvious slopers. Make sequential moves through edges to a jug. Power off the jug through large slopers, past a pinch and undercling to an easy topout. (V3) (SS TO)

a. **Shroomin': Start several feet left of the *Mushrooms* problem on a jug pinch. Move up and right past a sloper and jugs to join *Mushrooms* at the first sloper. (V2) (SS TO)

Past *Mushrooms* is a series of low-quality, chossy problems.

Dan Brayack getting high on *Mushrooms*.
PHOTO BY BOB ARTHUR

OTHER AREAS

Coopers Rock and the Morgantown area feature a plethora of other bouldering areas. These areas, and their respective qualities and access, are described here.

Coopers Rock Areas

All of these areas are open to bouldering.

1. Triangle Boulders: This area, located near the clay furnace, offers a host of moderately developed boulders. The approach (green briars from hell) and lack of trails, coupled with a low concentration of problems, did not warrant listing this area.

2. Lower Rock City: This area, located about a mile down the Ridge trail from the Picnic Table Boulder (Rock City signpost and shelter), offers about 30 high-quality problems interspersed among about five subareas. Classics in this area include *Purity of Essence* (V6) on the Incredibly Overhanging Wall, and *Cruelty to Animals* (V7) on the Top Secret Boulder.

3. Motorcycle Boulders: Located down from the Overlook toward Haystack is this small area with one classic problem and several other problems. The classic *Zygott* (V2) is the obvious pocketed line. It starts with a jump and ends with a thin mantel.

Other Morgantown Areas

1. Pioneer Rocks: This bouldering area, located on Route 7, is located on private property. Though access in the past has not been an issue, there are several strict rules that everyone must follow in order to secure bouldering privileges.

• *Absolutely no dogs.* Leave your smelly mutt at home. The landowner has a dog and access is currently threatened because of a tangle between the owner's dog and a climber's dog.

• *Pioneer Rocks is closed during hunting season, bottom line.* The landowner is an avid hunter and will close the area if climbers interfere with his hunting.

• *Do not litter.* If you see litter, pick it up, no questions.

2. Commando Boulders: Once thought to be in Coopers Rock State Forest, it turns out that this area is located on private property. Avoid bouldering here.

3. Army Rocks: A popular rappelling area that is also located on private property.

4. Woodland Walls: Permanently closed to climbing—do not come here.

5. Darnell Hollow: This "locals" area is located within the CRSF boundaries. The bouldering here is not very good. People generally dump dead deer and garbage here. Access does not seem to be a problem.

ROUTES BY GRADE INDEX

INDEX

ABOUT THE AUTHORS

Dan Brayack was introduced to climbing at age twelve when his grandmother (a registered belayer) took him to a Pittsburgh climbing gym. His passion intensified when he moved to West Virginia to study civil engineering. Although he prefers sport climbing, he loves bouldering—especially technical slab and face. He now lives in Fayetteville, West Virginia.

PHOTO COURTESY OF DAN BRAYACK

Born in California, Tim Keenan began climbing while attending West Virginia University, where he studied apparel design. He honed his skills at Coopers Rock and enjoys all things sandstone, preferring roofs, bulges, and slightly overhung faces with bad holds. He has traveled to Alabama, New York, and France, but he considers Coopers Rock his home.

PHOTO © DAX SOMMERFELD/DAXOPUS.COM

ACCESS: IT'S EVERYONE'S CONCERN

The Access Fund is a national nonprofit climbers' organization working to keep climbing areas open and conserve the climbing environment. Need help with a climbing related issue? Call us and please consider these principles when climbing.

- **ASPIRE TO CLIMB WITHOUT LEAVING A TRACE:** Especially in environmentally sensitive areas like caves. Chalk can be a significant impact. Pick up litter and leave trees and plants intact.
- **MAINTAIN A LOW PROFILE:** Minimize noise and yelling at the crag.
- **DISPOSE OF HUMAN WASTE PROPERLY:** Use toilets whenever possible. If toilets are not available, dig a "cat hole" at least six inches deep and 200 feet from any water, trails, campsites or the base of climbs. Always pack out toilet paper. Use a "poop tube" on big wall routes.
- **USE EXISTING TRAILS:** Cutting switchbacks causes erosion. When walking off-trail, tread lightly, especially in the desert on cryptogamic soils.
- **BE DISCRETE WITH FIXED ANCHORS:** Bolts are controversial and are not a convenience. Avoid placing unless they are absolutely necessary. Camouflage all anchors and remove unsightly slings from rappel stations.
- **RESPECT THE RULES:** Speak up when other climbers do not. Expect restrictions in designated wilderness areas, rock art sites and caves. Power drills are illegal in wilderness and all national parks.
- **PARK AND CAMP IN DESIGNATED AREAS:** Some climbing areas require a permit for overnight camping.
- **RESPECT PRIVATE PROPERTY:** Be courteous to landowners.
- **JOIN THE ACCESS FUND:** To become a member, make a tax-deductible donation of $35.

P.O. Box 17010
Boulder, CO 80308
303.545.6772

ACCESS FUND
your climbing future
www.accessfund.org